I Hope
I Screw
This Up

How Falling In Love with Your Fears Can Change the World

Kyle Cease

NORTH STAR WAY

new york   london   toronto   sydney   new delhi

North Star Way
An Imprint of Simon & Schuster, Inc.
1230 Avenue of the Americas
New York, NY 10020

First North Star Way hardcover edition May 2017

NORTH STAR WAY and colophon are trademarks of Simon & Schuster, Inc.

For information about special discounts for bulk purchases, please contact Simon &
Schuster Special Sales at 1-866-506-1949 or business@simonandschuster.com.

The North Star Way Speakers Bureau can bring authors to your live event.
For more information or to book an event contact the North Star Way Speakers
Bureau at 1-212-698-8888 or visit our website at www.thenorthstarway.com.

Manufactured in the United States of America

10 9 8 7 6 5 4

Library of Congress Cataloging-in-Publication Data is available.

ISBN 978-1-5011-5209-2
ISBN 978-1-5011-5220-7 (ebook)

Contents

Foreword

The late, heart-centered comedian Robin Williams once said, "Comedy is acting out optimism." Mark Twain put it this way: "Humor is mankind's greatest blessing." It's no wonder, then, that Kyle Cease began his professional career as a comedian, for as is abundantly evident throughout this book, his optimism and humor are highly effective medicines for the human spirit. If there is one outstanding truth among the many within these pages, it's that one's calling in life is an ever-evolving expression of oneself. It is this realization that inspired Kyle to turn deeply within and shine the searchlight on how to deliver his gifts, talents, and skills as a source of inspiration and encouragement to his readers, as well as those who attend his Evolving Out Loud events. Through written expression of his personal growth, Kyle vulnerably shares with us how he came to combine humor with transformation, which has become a healing tool for millions of individuals.

Great teachers, such as the Buddha, many Hindu sages, and Jesus, to name a few, have encouraged us to be fully present in the now-moment, to remain attentive, awake, and aware. And for good reason, for it is being *mindfully conscious*—not self-conscious, which is ego-related—that stands us before the cosmic mirror in which we can catch the reflection of our Original Face. When through these means we cultivate the courage to look straight into ourselves, we become the calm, wise seer of our true life path. And just as it did for Kyle, the mind chatter of childhood conditioning falls away as we begin to dis-identify with its emotional noise and stop catering to its demands. At first this can feel like unfamiliar territory, causing us to ask, "Is this the real me?" But when our analytical mind stops defining the boundaries of who we think we are or who we should be, the deepest and most authentic Self begins to emerge.

The encouragement you will receive from Kyle's personal journey begins with the wisdom of no longer rejecting parts of yourself, with embracing with loving-kindness that you are the vast space of consciousness that holds it all. Feelings of fear, sadness, anxiety—when they are not rejected and instead experienced for the self-revelations they offer—no longer are regarded as enemies but rather as signposts guiding us to the next step in our evolutionary growth. We then begin to welcome all the beauty of what it means to be alive and all the pure, creative intelligence and unconditional love that is our inheritance.

I share from personal experience that when Kyle speaks at the Revelation Conference, which is hosted by the Agape International Spiritual Center, the organization I founded, the energy in the room is vibrant with joy; it becomes filled with authentic soul-laughter. The self-awareness into which he escorts us will also escort you, dear reader, into a deep intimacy with yourself.

Michael Bernard Beckwith
Author of *Spiritual Liberation and Life Visioning*
February 22, 2017, Los Angeles, California

Introduction

Ladies and Gentlemen, allow me to introduce this book. This book, ladies and gentlemen.

chapter 1

Start Reading Here

So here's the deal, I'm scared shitless right now. I'm two sentences into a sixty-thousand-word book that I think I need to write because my manager, Norm, says my career won't really take off until I have a book. I got a deal from a huge publisher because they saw me perform and loved how I was able to walk onstage and speak my absolute truth to a crowd of strangers while making them laugh at the same time. I signed the deal and everything was going great until they said, "Okay, now write a book."

If you think I wrote that because it's a funny way to start a book, you're wrong. Right now I'm in a battle with my mind, which is trying to do everything it can to stop me from writing so it can escape the pain I feel in my chest as I type. My mind is trying to tell me that I don't know how to do this. It's telling me that this book is going to suck. It's telling me I'm going to miss my deadline and reminding me of a Facebook comment where someone said my vocabulary was atrocious, and once I understood what that meant, I was really hurt. The thought that I have to write this book with the English skills of a twelve-year-old has been standing between me and my happiness for the last six months.

So far, I've started this book about a dozen times. I tried writing with cowriters, I tried writing alone, I tried writing in restaurants, I tried going to a cabin in Monterey. I almost tried not writing the book at all. I basically forgot everything I've ever discovered about creativity and let *how* I was going to write this book get in the way of *why* I'm writing this book, which I'm in the process of figuring out.

Here's a picture of me as I try to write this. As you can see by how high my hair is, I'm having a hard time.

And now I'm thinking about you. You spent twenty bucks, hopefully thirty, on this book with the hope that it would help you in some way, and the first page is just about how scared I am to write it. I'm sorry, the only thing I know how to do is say exactly what's on my mind. I know that might sound strange, but what's stranger to me is the fact that most people *don't* say what's actually on their minds. We're always thinking something, but instead of saying what we're really thinking, which would free us and open us up to new possibilities, we instead say what we think people want to hear. How much easier would life be if we just said what we were thinking in the moment?

You would have sensed my inauthenticity immediately if I was feeling fear in every ounce of my body and I just overlooked it in order to write the "right" thing. Instead, by baring my soul and telling you what I'm actually experiencing, I'm freeing myself from the pain I would otherwise be hiding and holding on to. Something I've learned is that sharing my deepest truth, no matter how scary it is in the moment, is freedom. My only pain would come from *repressing* that truth.

For instance, if a man were to get in an elevator and there was a beautiful woman next to him, he might be trying to think of something to say to her to open up a conversation. What if he just said that? What if he turned to the woman and said, "I'm trying to think of the right thing to say to you." Think of how honest, vulnerable, and freeing that would be. Instead of hiding behind some cheesy pickup line, he gives her his heart, his fears, his truth, and he opens up the possibility for her to do the same. Wouldn't it be attractive if someone started a conversation with that level of authenticity? It brings out a mystery, it opens your mind, it speaks to your heart. It's not a corny line; it's actually true. It gives you the opportunity to respond because now you're playing catch with a possibility. You could respond with "Well, you could start out by talking about how nice my hair is." So now you have a conversation that's playful and freeing you from your fears because you're taking your truth and putting it out there.

Most people don't do that though. Most people get on the elevator and see the attractive person and go, "It sure is weather outside today." And then the other person goes, "Yes, and there was weather yesterday too." Now both of them aren't speaking from their hearts. They're speaking from a place of strategy because they're trying to get something from each other. They're not being real with their feelings; they're salesmen. You would never look in the mirror and say to yourself, "The weather is nice." You would talk about your fears and what is really going on at the deepest level. When you're totally honest and transparent about what you're thinking, you free yourself from it.

So I guess what I'm hoping for here is that whoever might be reading this will be able to connect to me and what I'm experiencing if I just share exactly what I'm going through. I know you may not necessarily be in the middle of trying to write a book, but you might be able to connect on the idea that I feel like I need to do something a certain way to make someone else happy. Have you ever felt that way? Have you felt that you had to do something that wasn't what you really wanted to do, just to get love or approval from a friend, a teacher, a boss, a spouse, a parent? Do you know what I mean? Can you feel me? ARE YOU THERE?

See? This is why I do better with audiences. I have no idea who the hell is reading this and how you're reacting. I guess that's why I'm in so much fear right now. Like most people, I've been trained to try to make everyone around me happy so I can feel loved by them. I was trained to do that so well that I did it professionally as a national touring comedian for twenty years. By writing this book, I'm actually learning how much I've been addicted to other people's opinions of me. This is both scary and exciting. It's scary to realize that, but it's exciting to uncover something that I never knew about myself before. I'm doing exactly the same thing I do when I'm on-stage, but because I don't see you nodding and laughing, it makes me think I'm not doing a good job and I won't be loved. I guess that's what is really happening here and why I've had such a hard time starting this. I'm trying to make my manager, my publisher (Hi, Michele, do you like it?), and everyone else happy instead of connecting to why I'm *really* writing this book.

I'm not writing it for any of them, and to be honest, I'm not even doing this for you. This might *seem* like a book that I made for you, but the reality is that you are the muse for me as I continually evolve into my soul. I know I have to write this book because my experience has shown me that if I'm in this much pain, then there is something really important that I need to learn. I've had many times where I really felt like bailing on something that I was afraid of, but when I stuck with it, it caused me to grow internally and turned out to be the greatest decision I ever made. I know that as I stay in the room and begin to just accept all these fears and emotions, I'll begin to transcend my addiction to "doing a good job" and move into a version of myself that is freer than I have ever been.

Maybe you're in pain too. Maybe that's why you picked up this book. Maybe hearing someone face the deepest truth in themselves will awaken something in you, and you will be able to access a new level of freedom too . . . but the moment I take that into consideration, I won't be giving my gift to its fullest. Why? Because I'll be thinking more about what you want and how to make my audience happy than truly allowing whatever words want to come through. I just have to surrender to whatever results come out of that place so I can truly tap into the edge of my creation. This book will be much better if I let go of any outcome.

Think of an apple tree. An apple tree is just here to make apples. Apple trees don't care if we like their apples or not. They don't care if we make apple juice, applesauce, or apple mayonnaise with their apples. Apple trees aren't ever thinking, "How many apples will I sell?" or "What will I get for these apples?" If they did care, they'd be so caught up worrying about the endless number of things that could happen to their apples that it would stifle their ability to make them. Even though there is a part of me that doesn't recommend that you make mayonnaise out of this book, I know I need to release myself from what you do with this information. I'm just here to make apples. Maybe by releasing any expectation of an outcome, I might be able to make ten times as many apples that taste even better because I'm slipping out of "What do I get?" and moving into "What am I here to share?" (or, if you want to go deeper: "What is trying to express itself through me?").

If I'm writing this to make anyone else happy outside of myself, then I'll be capped at the level of their expectation and miss out on the infinite amount of creativity and unknown possibilities that could come from this. Anyone who has made a true impact on this planet, at one point, had to step out of the expectation of the people around them and listen to an inner calling that moved them into a place of originality beyond what they had done before. Like that point, for example . . . that just made so much sense to me and unlocked something inside of myself, and I have never said it before. If I had just started writing a typical self-help book with a bunch of great concepts instead of sharing the actual pain I was experiencing, I never would have written that sentence. Man, that sentence was good. Well, looks like we're done here. How many words is that so far? Crap, it's only 1,839. It truly felt to me like 22,910. I thought for sure I was almost done. This is insane, what am I doing???

Okay, well, I guess I can look at what's happened so far and realize this has already gotten a little easier. My body is letting go of some of the tension that was making this so difficult and I already know a little more than I did when I started, so by the end of this I'll probably be totally on fire and will have an entirely new level of awareness to share with you. If it's only been an hour since I started, then what might happen ten hours from now? Now my emotions are moving from 100 percent fear to, let's say, 50 percent fear, 49 percent excitement, and 1 percent horny. I'm kind of getting aroused by my work. But only 1 percent, so don't bother coming over. I have to get up early anyway.

Any time we start something creative, it's kind of like turning on a garden hose for the first time in a while. The water that comes out first is dirty and gross, but once that's out of the way, what comes next is some sweet, sweet, garden-hose tap water. So all I've done so far is start to get that dirty water moving to make way for some delicious garden-hose water. I think I made that analogy confusing, because halfway through I realized that garden-hose tap water is still not good water. A more accurate analogy would be that hopefully this book is going to start as dirty garden-hose water and end up as crystal-clear Himalayan springwater that frees you from your mind prison.

Okay, now I'm starting to have fun and these pages are starting to turn into a playground. I'm slowly starting to slip out of the self-imposed rules I had put on what this book is supposed to be and what is acceptable for a book about transformation. I had in my head a vision of what the book should look like that wasn't coming from my heart, it was coming from a mental projection of what I thought was expected of me. I started thinking that it had to be like all the other books, which would actually stop me from being original. Now that I feel like I'm stepping out of that cage, I'm seeing all sorts of possibilities for where this could go. Like maybe one chapter could be a scratch-and-sniff chapter. Okay, bad example, but the point is, the doors are opening and ideas are starting to come through. There is still fear for sure though, like after I came up with that scratch-and-sniff idea, my mind was like, "That is so stupid, words don't have smells." But now I'm telling you about that thought, so I'm free again!

PS: I just thought of a word that has a smell. The word is "moisture." What do you think that word smells like? My friend Dan says, "Moldy sponge." I say, "Rotten orange." But it turns out the word "moisture" smells like fresh waffles with motor oil and leaves.

I just realized that I don't even know why I think writing sixty thousand words is such a big deal. Hold on, I'm going to Google how many words we usually speak in an hour. Holy crap. (Thanks for holding, by the way.) I found out we would average somewhere between ten thousand and twelve thousand words per hour if we talked nonstop. That's really exciting to me because I do events where I speak onstage for two days straight. I literally walk onstage without any idea what I'm going to say and then speak from my heart for like eight hours a day, both days. The only preparation I do is to relax and play in every moment leading up to the event so that when I'm onstage, the only difference is I'm three feet higher. If I can talk for two entire days in front of thousands of people, this is nothing.

What I feel happening now is that my mind is starting to get evidence that it's not going to die from doing something that it hasn't done before and is starting to get on the same page as the creative, apple-tree part of me that wants to express itself. Now I'm at 62 percent excited, 35 percent scared, and 3 percent horny, so let's play tonight by ear. I can feel my mind piling on all the reasons why this is going to be fun and easy instead of giving me evidence of why I'm a terrible person with an elementary school child's vocabulary. That would be scrampulent. (Just because I don't know all of the words, that doesn't mean I can't make words up.) It wouldn't only be scrampulent, it would be markoviltly scrampulent.

The moment that we do the thing is when we learn how to do the thing. I feel like I read that somewhere or have said it before or something, or maybe I just saw it on a bumper sticker. I wonder if it's plagiarism if I spend a paragraph debating on whether I wrote it or not.

Anyway, I think it fit the moment, so I'll keep it for now and ask my editor later. If you're reading this, that means either that I actually did come up with it or that plagiarism is fine if you question it right after.

Where was I? Oh yeah, I was going to say our minds are always trying to figure out how something is going to go, but they can only project what will happen in the future based off of what's happened in the past. Almost all of us see ourselves as our *past stories*. We believe that our identities are contained within the boundaries of what we've accomplished, what we've failed to accomplish, what we've looked like, what we've learned, etc. Anything outside of what we've experienced before is threatening to the identities we've had our entire lives.

From speaking on thousands and thousands of stages, changing careers from a successful stand-up comedian to an unknown transformational speaker, and constantly making leaps that seem really scary, I've learned that when we haven't done something before, our minds are under the illusion that we can't, so they're horrified that we're moving beyond the story they have built to protect us. Can you feel what I mean by that? Here's an example: If you think "who you are" is someone who makes $20,000 a year and then someone offers you a million dollars, then to your mind, that's actually dangerous. It's very possible that you might sabotage that opportunity, subconsciously trying to protect the limited story that you came from. This is why many instant lottery winners go broke.

Many people get a lot of love and connection from their limited stories. We learn that when we're depressed, when we're stressed, or when we're having a hard time, people are there to comfort us. Often that makes thriving, becoming successful, and changing really scary. Most of us would admit that we may be afraid of failure to some degree, but many of us might not even be aware that we are just as afraid of success. Your identity thinks that if you succeed, you're going to be something different than you are now and the limited story that you've been identifying with is going to die. It's actually saving its life by not letting you succeed.

When I booked the movie *10 Things I Hate About You* and moved from Seattle to Los Angeles, I lost a lot of friends who thought I was "going Hollywood." Some of my first experiences with success made me think that maybe I'd rather stay small and safe than risk it for the unknown. Had I listened to that voice that wanted to keep me small, I might not have experienced the massive growth I've gained by constantly moving toward my edge or been given the opportunity to learn that true friends will love me unconditionally. We don't know if we're going to get love in the same way we're used to if we're successful, so our minds often pull us back into circumstances that are comfortable and familiar, even if they don't match the life we really want.

For me, writing this book, and living on the edge of my heart as I do it, is competing with my protective story that says I'm not an author, and right now every word I type is slowly, and a little painfully, undoing that false belief. As I keep going, I know I'll realize more and more that I'm not my past story—in fact, I'm not any story, I'm just this moment, and the more I release those limitations, the more I will begin to open up to possibility and make room for an entirely new perspective on myself to come through.

This book is literally me giving myself advice, and I'm realizing that the true reason I'm writing it is to move past my own fears, tap into an infinite oil well of understanding, and put into practice everything that I learn in the process . . . and by the way, as you read this, feel free to take only the things that feel good to you and let go of anything that doesn't. Hell, I won't even take all the advice in this book. I haven't written it yet, but what if some of it sucks? I mean, a ton of it's going to be good—and be open-minded—but also do research within yourself to find what feels right for you.

This isn't about me telling you how to change your life, this is me giving a megaphone to my inner voice and as a result, maybe you'll give yourself permission to start listening to yours. As we go deeper, we might end up finding out that they're actually all coming from the same place. That might be too deep for chapter one, but the unlimited source of infinite possibility that lives within me wanted to say it, so screw it.

So, my job here is to work on me even more than I work on the book . . . whatever ends up on the page will be just a by-product of the internal growth that will come from shedding the things that have been keeping me small and from stepping into the highest version of myself that I have ever been.

I can feel a guidance that is trying to pull me into a new way of being, and if I actually take the advice that is coming through me, a new layer of possibility will reveal itself. Or, in other words, as I go deeper into the onion of who I am, I'll find the tomato at the center of that onion and will be able to make a delicious onion-and-tomato sandwich. I'm not good at metaphors. My metaphors are like the chocolate mint on a hotel pillow: when you want to go to sleep, you have to either eat it and brush your teeth again, or just move it to the nightstand and eat it tomorrow.

I know that just because I haven't done this before doesn't mean that I can't access the ability to write an amazing book. We all have the exact same level of ability to tap into the unlimited creativity available in every moment.

If you realize you're just this moment, then you are infinite possibility. You, me, Obama, Oprah, and a homeless person . . . we're all the same. We're all just heart and lungs and infinite potential. The only thing that separates you from any human being is your belief in your past story; other than that, we're all the same. When we stop using our limiting stories as barriers to the outside world and other people, we start to discover an entirely new type of collaboration with life that is effortless, inspired, and open-ended.

Look, I'm feeling much better!

As you can probably tell from the picture, I'm starting to get really excited to keep writing this book and to learn what I need to learn. I hope you're excited to stay with me, because something tells me a lot of potential, a huge amount of opportunity, and tons of new possibilities are going to be uncovered along the way. I know "potential," "opportunity," and "possibility" are almost the same word, but I felt like I needed a lot of emphasis in that sentence because this chapter is almost over, and I wanted it to feel exciting for you because my mind still cares a little what you think. I also don't have a mextrimal amount of words to describe what could happen.

Maybe this book will show us what happens when we step up, create from our heart, and start learning how to love every part of ourselves. Maybe it'll show us what it's like to drop our resistance to life and live in total flow. Maybe it'll accidentally help us minimize anxieties, addictions, codependencies, and other fears. I seriously don't know. And even though that's probably scary for both of us, I know that on the other side of that fear is a freedom that will bring both you and me more into alignment with our naturally creative, unconditionally loving, and effortlessly playful selves. I'm honored to be on this journey with you.

So, there it is, chapter one. The result of walking into my fear, staying in the room, and being okay with not knowing. Welcome.

chapter 2

The Second Chapter of This Book

Before I do anything, I think it's worth pointing out that I don't actually know why we're on a new chapter now. If you and I were having a conversation, I wouldn't make a good point and then say, "And now for chapter two." So I guess I'm just doing this because every book I've read, or at least started/pretended to read, or books that I have bought and lost/accidentally eaten some pages from/put into the laundry/used as a booster seat, has had chapters in it. I don't really know how chapters work or how I should be using them, but I guess I'll figure it out as we go.

Nothing like taking the time to wash and dry a good book.

chapter 3

The Six-Minute Alien Ab-duction

So, if you've read chapter one, which you probably have (since very few people start books on chapter two, and if you did on this book, you're going to be really confused), you might have noticed that it almost sounds like it was written by two different people. First, there's a version of me who is absolutely terrified and cares what people think, and then there's another version of me who has all the answers and is actually giving advice to the me who's afraid. How was there one me who had no idea what to do, and started off by saying I was scared shitless, and a few paragraphs later, another me showed up with all the solutions? Why did I shift from a scared little child with great abs into a wise, confident, strong man with great abs?

I believe there's this scared little kid in all of us who just hopes people will like them and wants to do a "good job." There's a part of us that thinks love and approval can only come from outside because that's how we were taught to get it as children. We learned that the way to get the approval we craved was to mold and shape our behaviors into whatever would get us a positive reaction from the people around us. Through years of jumping through hoops for parents, teachers, coaches, and friends, we started to live in the illusion that we need to look to others for our sense of connection and self-worth.

As a kid, my way of connecting with the people around me was through comedy, and I got a lot of love from my parents and family for being the center of attention and telling jokes. I created the idea in my mind that making a room full of people laugh meant I was loved and that I was "good." As a result, I still feel a little uncomfortable in a crowded room unless I'm onstage. The way that I got love in our family's living room in Bothell, Washington, in 1985 is still influencing parts of my behavior as a thirty-eight-year-old man with top-notch abs. How weird is that? We think we grow up into mature adults and move beyond that part of ourselves, but the truth is we just pile a bunch of crap on top of it and let it drive us around.

Imagine being dropped off tomorrow on another planet that's inhabited by a bunch of thirty-foot-tall giants. When you arrive, you're assigned to two of these giants, who are supposed to provide food and shelter and protect you from all the other giants for the next twenty years. One of the giants often comes home drunk and yells at you if you speak your opinion, so you learn to stay quiet to protect yourself. The other one gives you attention when you tap-dance, so you learn that's a way to get love. For two decades, you learn the way to get attention and avoid being hurt is by behaving the way your giants want you to. At the end of the twenty years, once you've mastered tap dancing and keeping your mouth shut, they kick you out into the world and you're on your own to fend for yourself among all the other giants.

The only thing you've learned about how to get what you need is what your giants taught you, so you keep going up to all these other giants and tap-dancing annoyingly in front of them and withholding your opinions and authentic self so they don't yell at you. The ways that you got what you wanted from your old giants doesn't translate to the rest of the world, so as you use all your old methods to get love and protect yourself, you can't understand why they're not working. Because the other giants on this planet don't like the way you've learned to behave, it's going to be really hard for you to survive.

This is exactly what happens to us as kids. The mind, whose primary goal is to keep us alive, starts to create a blueprint of how to avoid the wrath of these giants, which are our only source of well-being, and then we stay locked in that blueprint from then on. The need for food and shelter becomes the need for love and approval as we move deeper into the illusion that our happiness comes from someone or something outside of ourselves. Even once we're adults and providing food and shelter for ourselves, we're still constantly looking for someone, anyone, outside of us to take on the role of the provider of our love and well-being. Someone who will tell us we're good. That we're loved. It's a matter of survival.

When I started chapter one, that part of me was going crazy. I was afraid that I would fail. To the child in me who has created the false belief that failing means I won't be loved, the idea of taking the risk of doing something I've never done before was a life-and-death situation. And so, like anyone might do on the verge of death, I freaked out a little.

Some of you might be thinking that writing a book isn't a life-and-death situation and that I should stop being such a baby with incredible eight-pack abs, but that's exactly the point. When we live in that fearful part of ourselves, all sorts of stuff that isn't really that big of a deal completely starts to feel like it's life-and-death. Filing our taxes, going to a job interview, asking someone out on a date, throwing out that autographed *Back to the Future* poster that we've had since we were a kid and even though we have no need for it, we really really want to keep it . . . those are all things that we've created stories around in our mind that have linked us back to that fight-or-flight response in our instinctual nervous system. Our minds are constantly putting us in survival mode all day so they can protect us from what they think will be death, and unfortunately, our minds think almost everything is death. Our minds think starting something new is death. They think being judged by other people is death. They think losing a friend is death. If you're wrong about something, that's death. If you're not number one, if you get made fun of, if you don't make enough money, you'll die. Your mind even thinks throwing out an old shirt is death, so instead you keep that shirt that's been hanging in your closet for five years without ever being used in case you ever need to go to a Bon Jovi concert again.

So, we're constantly doing things unconsciously to avoid dying. We judge people before they can judge us. We hold on to relationships and friendships that don't fulfill us anymore. We hoard as much money as possible. We avoid following our passions and stay small. We keep going to Bon Jovi concerts, even though the tour dates on our Bon Jovi T-shirts are from five years ago. Every addictive pattern you might have in your life is because of the illusion that the only way to avoid death and find love is to search for something outside of yourself.

For me, I first connected the idea of being loved to getting approval externally through other people, and that was just the gateway drug to getting love externally from things, experiences, and situations or outcomes. Our minds will try to get that sense of love and connection from all types of things when they become desperate. In the absence of love from people, we can find what we think is a temporary feeling of love from things like food, television, drugs, alcohol, clothes, cars, money, success, achievement. These are all just shallow replacements for what we're actually looking for though: motorcycles. Wait, I got confused. What we're actually looking for is *love*. Motorcycles are what my dad loves . . . a lot.

It's this seeking-love part of us that just wants to eat ice cream all day and scroll through Facebook looking for some type of connection, even though we just end up being shown all the new people our exes are dating and the parties we didn't get invited to.

In the end though, getting love from people, possessions, food, achievement . . . it's all just a symptom of that fundamental belief that love is found outside of ourselves. It's only this small, fearful part of ourselves that thinks it is separate from the love that is the core of our being. All we are is love. More on that later though . . .

So what do I call that fearful part of us that is addicted to external love and afraid of failure? If you're one of those people with a stack of Deepak Chopra books on your shelf, you might assume that the scared version of us is what he would probably call the "ego." (One thing you missed out on by reading this book instead of seeing me in person is that if you were seeing me live onstage, I probably would have said "ego" with a really great impersonation of Deepak Chopra that would have gotten a huge laugh. I'm funnier in person. I'll be sure to tell you all the other things you're missing out on by reading this book too; my publisher will probably think that's a great idea. One thing that comes to mind is Netflix. By reading this book you're missing out on watching Netflix.)

I don't really call it that though. The word "ego" is kind of like the word "God" to me. Every person has a totally different definition that they've created for this invisible, indescribable phenomenon. Just like how some people see God as a fiftysomething white male with a temper, the word "ego" is just as loaded. This book has nothing to do with religion. You can read this and be a Christian, a Buddhist, or an atheist, or follow any religion. Now I feel like if I don't list every religion someone will be offended. There's a part of me that wants to write a list of every religion in the world just because it would be funny, but I realize that will take way too much effort for way too little a payoff.

Even though it doesn't matter what you call it, and what we're talking about is an invisible thing that can't fully be defined anyway, there's a ton of names for what some people call that aspect of ourselves and even more descriptions of what people think it is. Here's a list of things people have called it:

the ego
the mind
the head
the small self
your identity
Michael Douglas
Glenn Close
Anne Archer

Those last three aren't really names people use for it, they're just actors from the movie *Fatal Attraction*. I figure if a lot of people are going to be jumping back and forth between this and Netflix, I should probably ease the transition a little by offering a few movie recommendations. If you haven't seen it, it's a classic and currently has a 78 percent fresh rating on Rotten Tomatoes.

I've used pretty much all of those terms at one point or another, but the ones I think I use the most are "the head" and "the mind." I probably use those the most just because they give me an actual, physical place in my body that I can relate to. When I'm in fear, judgment, or self-doubt, I can literally feel my awareness move out of my whole body and into my head. When you're in your head, you're always trying to strategize a way to avoid "death."

Turn the page for a graphic of where I feel it when I'm in my head.
It's probably pretty obvious, since everyone knows what a head is,
but just so no one gets left out.

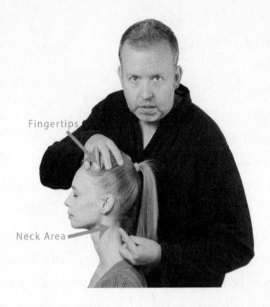

I mean, if they still have to tell us what a seat belt is when we get on an airplane, I guess some people still might not know what a head is. The head is near the fingertips, above the neck area.

When I'm trying to "figure something out" or stressing, I actually feel the tension of being locked inside the cage of my mind. Have you ever felt that? Have you ever noticed the shift between feeling free and wide open, and then all of a sudden being pulled into your head by a worry or stressful thought?

In the beginning of chapter one, I was completely trapped in my head and was limited to the perspective of my past story. You might have even felt in *your* head at the beginning of chapter one because we can only relate to something at the level it was created at. A song or a beautiful painting that was created while the artist was inspired and connected to their heart has the ability to pull us straight into our hearts as well. We don't know why, but somehow we can feel the depth in it.

As I continued to share exactly what I was feeling and began tapping into my creativity, I started to feel myself move out of my head and into more of a feeling of openness. Right now, even though my mind is still monitoring what I'm doing a little bit and bringing up fears here and there, I'm mostly feeling playful and loose and excited to do this book exactly how I want to, without thinking about how anyone else wants me to write it. One way that I moved into that place was by imagining that I'm not even publishing this book, that I'm just doing it for fun and as an exercise to pull me deeper into my creativity. Without the pressure and fear of what this book might mean, it feels like my mind has less to hold on to and protect against and is starting to let go a little bit.

As my mind starts to release its hold on me, I'm moving more into a second version of myself that is totally free and has nothing to worry about. This part of me isn't trying to re-create the kind of love and approval I got as a kid because it's already overflowing with unconditional love. I notice that when I'm in flow or in a heightened state of creativity, I actually begin to lose my addictions and become totally content in the moment. I actually am more fulfilled in my creativity than any person or accomplishment could ever make me feel.

It's like there's this part of ourselves that doesn't see itself through the lens of what we've done in our pasts; it somehow can see way beyond all of that and knows that what we are is just endless possibility. This has been proven to me over and over throughout the thousands of live performances I've given. There's no way that my rational mind could have ever planned some of the magic that has happened onstage through spontaneous moments. Like the time I made myself a salad during my act and ate it for twenty minutes because, for some reason, they put the stage in front of a salad bar . . . or the time that I decided to go onstage in my pajamas . . . or the time I invited a heckler onstage and then helped him decide to pursue his dream of becoming America's premier Meat Loaf impersonator. I know it sounds like I made that last one up, but I swear that happened. Like I said, there's something so much more intelligent than my mind that is guiding everything and making it turn out better than I ever could have planned.

It's almost as if this second part of us is connected to a perspective that is beyond time and can actually see the path that is in front of us, even though we can't. In this place, the logic and reasoning of the mind start to give way to intuition and guidance. The mind might never understand why *falling in love with not knowing* is one of the greatest ways to access this place of trust, and it doesn't have to understand.

When someone runs into a burning building to save a child, it's that part of them at work. It's not their mind calculating the risk and reward of the situation, it's something beyond them that is moving from a place of absolute knowing and selflessness. This part of ourselves is actually working for the benefit of the whole instead of just the individual. And from what I'm discovering, I believe it's the place that we were designed to live in. Collaboration, compassion, and possibility should be our normal resting place instead of something we only tap into when we rescue babies from burning buildings.

There are a ton of made-up names that people have used to label this second part of us over the years too:

heart
body
soul
higher self
God (not the angry one)
Nick Stahl
Marisa Tomei
Tom Wilkinson
Sissy Spacek

In the critically acclaimed film *In the Bedroom*, a young man (Stahl) falls for an older woman (Tomei). His disapproving parents (Spacek and Wilkinson) are met with tragedy when the relationship takes a turn for the worse. The Fowlers are left to pick up the pieces and deal with the inevitable repercussions of their choices. It's rated 93 percent fresh on Rotten Tomatoes, but I'd only recommend this film if you enjoy movies that unfold in what seems to be slightly slower than real time.

Of all of those names that don't matter, the ones I use the most to describe the part of me that feels expansive and free are "heart" and "body" because those are the places where I actually experience those feelings. When I'm sharing my total and complete truth, I can feel a deep emotion in my chest, and I feel creativity moving through my entire body when I'm in flow onstage or making a video. I know that this part of us doesn't necessarily reside in our physical hearts and isn't necessarily limited to our bodies, but there's a general feeling and experience these words point to that represents what aspect of ourselves we're most identified with in the moment.

Here's a to-scale, accurate representation
of what I mean when I say my *body.*

My heart is the part of me that knows everything is going to be all right and has all the answers. This part of me is compassionate, honest, and excited to express myself in totally original and authentic ways twenty-four hours a day. It's always there waiting for me to access it. It knows that I'm always supported and is connected to a perspective that knows no matter what, I am loved.

As I wrote chapter one, my head was blocking my heart from coming through because it was trying to control the outcome of this book (in order to survive), but the head isn't the enemy. In fact, it's our job to access and love both the head and the heart at the same time. Our minds are brilliant tools we've been given to use in collaboration with the creativity of our hearts, but many of us are living exclusively from our heads and have cut off the infinite wisdom of our souls. Our brains are basically like midlevel employees who have convinced all the other employees that they're the boss, and now everyone's confused about who's steering the ship. We then go back and forth between brilliance and chaos on an almost moment-to-moment basis.

You've probably experienced this for yourself, right? There's a part of you that can't decide what restaurant to go to with someone you're dating, and another part of you that can sit with a friend who's going through a tough time and give them hours of the most amazing advice ever. Think about that. There is a you that is totally flustered with basic things, then there is another you that shows up when you see someone in pain and is able to say the most insightful things for hours and hours. You could have written a book with the things you said. In fact, have you ever given someone advice, and then *you* learned from the advice you gave?

If you have, then what you experienced was the limited version of you stepping out of the way as you entered a place of giving, which allowed that bigger part of you with all the answers to come through. A lot of times we give other people advice that is actually meant for us.

Friend seeking advice: I have a stomachache.

Me: I think you should break up with her.

Friend seeking advice: I'm single.

What I'm realizing *right now*, after years of trying to convince my friends to get out of relationships they're not in, is that I should break up with Amber. So, Amber, I'm sorry that it took so long to tell you and that you're finding out about it as you're reading this book, but we had a great time; it's not you, it's me. I'm sorry that even though I found this out as I was writing this book, I still waited until it was fully published to tell you.

After moving into a career where I'm pretty much full-time giving advice to people, I've learned that the wisdom that comes out when you're selflessly helping someone else is also truly the wisdom that you need to hear. As I said before, I know that the things that I'm sharing in this book are for me to learn too. That's why this is so freaking exciting. I'm on the edge of my seat waiting to find out what I'm going to learn next. Apparently, right now, I'm learning that Amber and I just don't work (sorry again, Amber).

So, how can we have this clarity and guidance in one moment but then be totally confused and fearful the next?

This second aspect of ourselves, which we can feel in our hearts and bodies, gives us guidance way beyond the intelligence of our minds. Even though the mind shows us words and pictures, the body can give us a flash of intuition that tells us everything we need to know about a decision instantly. We get a feeling of excitement in our bodies when an idea or new possibility shows up. It could be writing a book, leaving your job, or moving to another country. Whatever it is, in that moment when we feel alive and expansive, our bodies are giving us a preview of what will happen and how we might feel in the future if we act on that inspiration.

Okay, this feels kind of weird to just throw you an exercise, since we're like thirty pages into this book and you're probably not really sure if I know what I'm talking about yet, but let's just try something for a second, because I really want you to experientially feel what I'm talking about here:

Imagine for a second the idea of doing something big that would make you feel free and expansive in your body. Maybe it's taking a long trip to an exotic island. Maybe it's taking a month off work so you can just meditate and connect to yourself. Maybe it's starting that new business you've been wanting to create. Maybe it's ending a relationship that isn't fulfilling you anymore (Amber). Maybe it's starting a relationship by telling that person how you feel finally (Christy). Maybe it's forgiving someone who hurt you. Maybe it's forgiving yourself for hurting others. It's probably the thing that you're afraid of. It's the thing that makes you almost want to close this book because you know that going deeper might uncover something you've been pushing down for a long time. Even though it might be scary to the mind, stay with me, this is the thing that is going to give you your greatest growth if you face it head-on. What's that thing? What would that be like? Actually take a few moments to think about what it would feel like to take that step that is on the edge of your comfort zone and how that would feel in your body. How would it feel to be the person who is actually moving toward that thing that calls to you?

If you can't feel anything or nothing exciting comes up for you, it could be that you're so used to moving from your mind that you don't even know that part of you exists. It's possible that you've lived for so long listening to what other people want you to do that you've been almost entirely cut off from that feeling of guidance. It's like working for forty years in an office where there's an elevator in the corner that you've never gotten on or even asked where it goes. Don't you want to find out where the hell it goes? If you just sit and listen to your body for long enough, sooner or later you'll get on that elevator and realize there's an entire building that you've never explored.

If you *were* able to get in touch with what that experience might be like, it's likely that you felt something in your body that felt expansive, and for a moment you might have felt totally free and excited. It's also likely that, for many of you, shortly after that feeling of expansion in your body, your mind snapped you back into "reality" with thoughts like "That'd be great, but who's gonna pay for it?" or "What if my business doesn't succeed?" or "What if they don't feel the same way?" You might have noticed the more excited you felt in your body, the more paralyzed you might have been in your mind. You probably could feel that feeling of expansion being sucked back into the confines of your head just as quickly as it began. If something like that happened to you, raise your hand.

Put your hand down, this is a book. I can't see you.

How many times have you had an idea that excited you and inspired all types of possibilities, until your mind came in and convinced you of all the reasons you couldn't do it? When that happens you can truly feel yourself split in two. One of you is listening to opportunity, one of you is listening to fear. You can feel the opportunity in your body and you can feel the fear in your mind. Which of those perspectives is true? Which perspective will you choose?

Through a countless number of experiences that have given me the chance to make that decision, I know that when you step into opportunity, you cut off the fear. When you step into fear, you cut off the opportunity. Which means, if you step into what your heart says, you cut off the worry of your mind. If you step into what your head says, you cut off the guidance of your heart. The decision to step into and take action toward anything in your life that excites you creates an entirely new vision of yourself and opens you up to more ideas and inspiration for what the next step might be. When you move from your mind, which believes you're just this limited person who can't move beyond their past, you get stuck with the same limited options that you've always had for what to do next. You don't have any limitations, you're just addicted to them. If you listen to the fear and *don't* move into action, you cut yourself off from the flow of creativity and the next step can't show up.

The mind can give you an elaborate and detailed list of reasons that you shouldn't do that thing you really want to do in your heart. It can tell you all of the people you might disappoint and how the numbers just might not add up. Your mind sees your worth only according to what you currently are, based on the evidence you have from your past instead of the potential of what you might become if you followed your calling. It knows only how to get love in the way you've gotten it before, so it tries to protect you by talking you out of the leap you're about to take. Your mind is so creative in the ways that it tries to keep you "safe" that it might even disguise itself by talking in the voice of one of your parents and tell you all the reasons they think you shouldn't do what your heart is pulling you toward. How insane is that? You can literally carry on a conversation with a mental projection of someone who isn't in the room with you, and that mental projection, which you created, will tell you all the reasons you shouldn't follow your dreams. We often listen to those fears because we're afraid of losing the love of our twenty-foot-tall alien parents who trained us into a way of getting love that seems to contradict what our calling might be.

All the heart can give you is a feeling. It doesn't have bar graphs and PowerPoint presentations like the mind; all it can do is say, "You know this feeling of excitement and passion? If you listen to me, you'll get more of this feeling, and when you have more of this feeling, you'll get even bigger ideas." Unfortunately, for many of us, the heart is much quieter than the mind, so we override the natural guidance that is in every cell of our being and listen to the short-sighted arguments the mind shouts at us.

If we think about the exercise you just did, your mind can probably fire off a thousand really good, substantial reasons that would show how bad of an idea it would be to do something like that. Even though the mind might be giving you tons of reasons to abandon that idea, if you felt a feeling of excitement or inspiration as you thought about it, there might actually be even more reasons why you *should* do it that you can't see right now. Basically, as my friend Diego said to me once, "You can always measure what you'll lose, but you can't see what you'll gain." He said that to me while I was debating whether or not to delete my Facebook account. It was really profound advice, but in case you're wondering, I still kept my account. Apparently Facebook is the one thing exempt from the guidance of my heart. Feel free to add me at www.facebook.com/kyleceasepage.

What if when you take that leap and start moving toward that thing that fills you with passion, you'll finally get to feel a freedom that you've been missing, get in touch with your heart, and start to appreciate life in a way that you haven't been lately? What if in that place of total connection with yourself, you come up with an idea for a book, a movie, or a new career that totally transforms your life and your income? If any of that happened, would you agree that the risk was worth the reward? Those are things the mind can't see based on your past that the heart might be trying to lead you to by showing you that feeling.

I'm not saying for you to go into debt right now so you can go on a vacation, or to just stop showing up for work. I can't tell you how many people have taken examples I've given literally and then gotten upset because it "didn't work." I'm not describing *how* to do anything. I'm writing all of this to show you that you already have the answers inside you that will naturally guide you into everything you want. This entire chapter is about listening to the calling within yourself instead of looking for external guidance. What I know to be true is that even though following that expansive feeling in our bodies can feel scary, if we take that leap into the unknown, an unlimited number of possibilities will show up to support us that we can't see before we've taken that leap.

Before I started writing this book I had no idea that I would say any of that. I had no idea that I'd be writing movie reviews in chapter three. All of that showed up as I took the first step and allowed the road to roll out in front of me. You don't need to know everything before you jump, you just have to know that it feels good deep down in your soul. Everything else is just speculation and distraction. I don't know how to end this chapter.

By the way, I just got off the phone with Christy and she said yes. I can't believe I almost continued my life with the fictional character named Amber that I made up for this chapter. That would have been a nightmare for all of us.

chapter 4

Extreme Progress

B ecause chapter three was so long, I figured that I'd make this one really short so you could feel like you're making progress with this book.

chapter 5

The Infinite Power of Sadness

As I start this chapter, I'm asking myself, what is the absolute deepest and most vital thing that I can share with you in this moment? What is on the very edge of my heart right now that wants to come out? Right now I'm just listening. I'm not trying to figure out what the logical next step is for this book. I don't have a list of concepts or principles that I'm trying to knock out in a certain order. If I did have that, it would get in the way of what is actually trying to happen. Everything truly creative that I've come up with in my life showed up in a moment of surprise; it didn't come from my trying to find the right way. I'm open to the suggestion of my heart because it knows way more than I do about what needs to be said in this book. To be totally honest, the most authentic thing I can share with you in this moment is the fact that I'm literally on the verge of tears as I write this.

This will probably be the funniest chapter so far.

Don't worry, nothing happened, everything's all right. I'm not sad in the way you might think. I didn't lose a puppy . . . I don't actually have a puppy to begin with, but that's not the reason I'm sad either. I'm also not sad because I've *never* had a puppy; I did have one once, and many other times. Even if I had never had one, that wouldn't be the reason I'm sad either. My point is, my sadness has nothing to do with puppies, at least directly. I've just been feeling and connecting to my heart over the past few days in a way that is radically different for me. As I said earlier, like a lot of people, I'm a master at calculating and adjusting to the needs of others, so I can often feel cut off from my heart when I'm around people. It has nothing to do with them, it's just the way I've been wired: to be the entertainer, the helper, the fixer. As much as I'm aware of the times when I'm overlooking my needs in order to keep other people happy, it can still be really easy for me to give up my own connection to satisfy others.

When I was a kid, my mom was my best friend. I talked to her about everything. In fact, she was the first person I told when I lost my virginity. She wasn't as excited about it as I was. And, because of how quickly it happened, neither was the woman I lost my virginity to.

Getting her love and approval (my mom [not the girl I lost my virginity to (in fact, it's because I didn't need her love and approval that she actually slept with me [the girl I lost my virginity to, not my mom (this is just to prove to you that I can come up with a fifth parenthesis)])])) was the highest thing I knew how to do, even though it wasn't always easy. I learned to make my connection to Mom my top priority, and maintaining that connection became more important than my connection to myself. As I've said before, when I left home, I found myself still searching for that love and approval from whoever happened to be in the room. I wanted to make sure everyone else was happy so I could re-create the same connection that I had with my mom.

Because I know that about myself, as I've been writing this book, I've been limiting the amount of contact that I'm having with other people so that I can really connect with the deepest calling within me. Seriously, I haven't even been talking to my team. I've actually been recording and sending them voice messages, like I'm in some kind of spy movie, so that I know everything I'm saying is totally true in my heart and not a compromise based on what I might assume people expect to hear. As I've been staying in this place of only listening to what my heart wants me to do, it's almost as if I'm shedding parts of myself that I didn't even know were there. I think that's actually where a lot of these raw emotions are coming from. It's as if I'm mourning the part of me that needed to get love externally from other people. It's kind of like when you're sad because you're going through a breakup. You might think you're sad because you're letting go of that person, but you're actually feeling sadness because you're letting go of who you were when you were with that person. There's some part of me that I'm saying good-bye to today.

Again, I'm realizing through the process of writing this book that this has truly been my greatest addiction. It's easy to recognize an addiction to drugs, alcohol, or food, but an addiction to getting approval from the outside world is a lot tougher to see, especially when it's what almost all of us have been trained to do since birth. We all have addictions like this that, many times, we have no idea are even there. An addiction is anything that you do that stops you from connecting to yourself. It's something that your mind wants to get so it can feel relief in the moment, but it keeps you from the unconditional love of your heart. An addictive action gives you short-term satisfaction, while following the guidance of your heart gives you actual, lasting fulfillment. Eating an entire carton of ice cream may satisfy your immediate craving, but it won't give you lasting fulfillment. Unless it's strawberry ice cream. Strawberry ice cream is 27 percent more fulfilling than other ice creams. Chocolate-chip mint and peppermint are second at 23 percent fulfillment. Then, weirdly, mango is at 20 percent, which upsets me because I think that mango tastes like soap.

If you were to just sit with your eyes closed for a moment any time you had an impulse to do something, you'd start to feel where that impulse was coming from. Right now, because I'm basically detoxing from external approval, I can feel in my head that I'd love to call up some friends and grab dinner or watch a movie with them. That's not a bad thing, but in this moment, the reason my mind wants to do that is so it can get love from them. This is one of the reasons we like to smoke cigarettes, drink alcohol, and eat unhealthy food when we're around other people. Our desire for external connection is so loud that we will sacrifice the health of our bodies just so we can get it. What I'm feeling in my heart and body is that I want to continue diving deeper into this so I can free myself from that addiction as I share it with you. So now I'm in a huge tug-of-war between my head and my heart. I know that I could get instant satisfaction if I went out with friends, but there is long-term growth and expansion if I stay with my heart and move deeper into the unconditional love that I am, which is way beyond any addiction.

My mind's first reaction to listening to my heart is to make me feel as much pain as it can so that I take the easy way out and find some kind of addiction for relief. If it's not its drug of choice, external approval, it'll take distraction . . . maybe some Netflix or Facebook will do the trick. Actually, I think there might be some chocolate in one of my cupboards. Maybe I'll just take a short break and eat some of that chocolate while I watch *Roseanne* on Netflix as I scroll through Facebook and wait on the nine pepperoni pizzas I just ordered.

The above paragraph is only an example of my mind reaching for distraction. None of that happened, but I might watch Roseanne *later. Although, many teachers believe watching* Roseanne *to be one of the main hurdles in true transformation:*

Remove Roseanne *to access full freedom.*

—LAO-TZU

Jackie from Roseanne *was hilarious, but peace is found within.*

—GANDHI

I don't care, let's just call it an iPhone. Now turn Roseanne *back on.*

—STEVE JOBS

What I'm discovering is, an addiction is just something we use to keep us from connecting to ourselves, from connecting to our souls. Whenever we make something more important than that connection, we're in an addiction. The reason an addiction causes so much pain and anxiety is just that it's separating us from the actual source of love and well-being that we have within us. This pain is a signal that we're moving further and further from our actual freedom. If we just listen to that pain and ignore the addictive impulses the mind is throwing at us, we can discover a new type of power and happiness that isn't dependent on our addictions to other people, situations, or substances. When we align with ourselves in the moment, our pain shifts to fulfillment and we're pulled toward thoughts and actions that expand us.

I'm saying "we" because I'm assuming you might be going through some of the same emotions that I am right now. As I'm discovering these hidden parts of myself, you might also be seeing things that you used to believe were "who you are" and are starting to realize that they're actually just parts of your past story. You might be uncovering some of the subtle addictions you didn't realize were causing you to disconnect from your heart. You might have made connections about the ways that you get love and are starting to feel that scared child in you who just wants to do things right.

Here is what I believe that sadness actually is: Our entire lives, we have used false, protective identities to help us move forward. These identities might not be our highest selves, but they were the highest that we knew at the time. These identities are not stable;

however, we have been living in those identities for so long that we feel that they are the safest thing to connect to.

It's like standing on a small, unstable iceberg for twenty years. The iceberg represents you in your protective state. The iceberg might be you controlling others. It might be you worrying. It might be you judging other people, etc.

Just by the simple action of reading this book, your awareness is growing. As it grows, you are discovering naturally that your identity is not that iceberg. Just by becoming more aware, you step off of the iceberg and onto actual, safe land. It's scary, because it's new, but it's actually much more safe and sturdy than the old iceberg. As you stand on the new land that you have discovered by accessing your heart, the iceberg of your protective story starts to float away.

Sadness is what happens when you keep trying to grab at the iceberg. It's floating away now. It was a part of you for twenty years or more. It's leaving. Just becoming aware that you are bigger than that false identity causes the iceberg to leave. There is nothing to do to get rid of it. It will go away on its own. Your tears are representing the death of the old story and you are saying good-bye to your old unstable life.

Sometimes it's not easy looking at those parts of ourselves, and as we've seen by my *Roseanne*-fueled-chocolate-binge example, sometimes they can make it scary as hell for us when we try to move beyond them. You might be feeling all sorts of emotions coming up as you start to give birth to a new vision of yourself. I'm right there with you. This is a never-ending process. That's probably not very comforting if you're feeling pain right now, so let me tell you this:

you and I are so lucky to know what we know. It would be so much worse to unconsciously hold on to this pain for the rest of our lives. Right now we're getting the opportunity to embrace our sadness so that we can transcend it and create room for an entirely new level of power to come through.

We're moving toward a time where more people than ever before are becoming aware of this, so we're actually dealing with the pain and sadness that have been stuffed down and passed on for generations and generations. It's like every generation has a trash bag full of fears and unconscious limiting beliefs that they haven't dealt with, which they hand to their children, and those kids grow up and just add to the bag, without throwing any of it out, and hand it to their kids. Each generation has not only handed down their new, heavier trash bag, but they believed they were the trash bag while they were holding it; that's why it's been so hard to let go of.

Think about the years and years of war, slavery, and plagues that our ancestors lived through without allowing themselves to acknowledge and transcend their sadness and pain. Right now some of the pain we might be subconsciously holding on to could just be the result of the fact that some distant relative in the 1700s didn't like cashews, but his dad made him eat them every day. His dad was a cashew farmer. That's why he was so insistent on his son eating cashews. You can probably tell I am eating cashews right now.

The point is, we have fears and beliefs clogging us up that have been passed down for generations . . . maybe even thousands and thousands of years. There is a lot of momentum behind some of the basic beliefs that we carry around, so sometimes releasing them is like stopping a moving train, which may or may not be transporting cashews. Just by the simple act of being with the pain, you are finally allowing centuries of handed-down pain to be released.

So it's no wonder I'm sad. I'm releasing parts of myself that are beliefs that have likely been passed down through several generations. For someone who's addicted to connecting to his mom, it's pretty tough to let go of a belief that was probably passed down to me by her and her parents. It's almost like I'm breaking off the family tree in a way. The family *cashew* tree, that is. I need to stop eating these.

I know it sounds weird to say that sadness is actually a good thing, but the societal lie is that it's better to be happy than to be sad. That's just a belief that our minds created. People always tell others things like "Be strong" and "Pull yourself up by your bootstraps," but what they don't realize is that one of the strongest things you can do is to actually feel the emotions that you're experiencing.

The truth is, none of our emotions are bad. Not sadness. Not fear. Not negativity. It's not about getting rid of our sadness, it's about becoming a big enough space that we can totally accept and love every part of ourselves. It's not about avoiding the dark and moving toward the light. The amount of light that we can bring into the world is equal to the amount of darkness that we can accept and love. We're not here to feel happy, we're here to feel fully. I'm really looking forward to seeing the Facebook memes that will be made from that quote.

This chapter is about sadness,
so here are a few sad pictures to help support my point.

Nickelback

I've come to learn that sadness is a time of growth. It's when I expand into the newest version of myself that I'm able to experience even more happiness than I ever have. Instead of sadness being a thing that I'm just supposed to avoid, I've come to learn that sadness is my teacher. I'm not saying sadness is better than happiness either, but there is a depth to sadness that happiness doesn't have. It forces you to look inward and truly appreciate the things you have in life. If you think about it, a happy, feel-good movie doesn't really make you appreciate life the same way that a sad movie does. After a sad movie, you walk out of the theater and are so grateful just to be alive. After a happy movie you just want to eat a bunch of cheeseburgers. That comparison isn't to scale . . . or even accurate . . . or true at all; you can have a massive amount of insight from a happy movie too. The point I'm making is that there's something about experiencing sadness that changes us, that expands us, that renews us. Being happy is great, of course, but it's the low moments of our lives that give us the insight and tools to thrive during the high moments.

What if we started to look at our "negative" emotions differently? I know we've been taught that we need to strive for happiness all the time, but what if embracing the entire spectrum of our emotions is the key to unlocking a level of well-being that is way beyond the limited scope of happiness?

I can remember a time when I was sitting on a plane and feeling pain because I was thinking about letting someone go who had been a huge part of my life (not Amber, she's fictional). I sat with this huge pain that I had been dealing with for a while and then just started crying. As soon as I let go enough to let those emotions through, I felt this huge release and a new power on the other side. I had been holding on to this pain for a while, years actually . . . and all it took was a couple of minutes of accepting it, then about thirty seconds of tearing up, and then it was gone. After about three minutes of truly facing and accepting this pain I had been holding on to, I was able to access an entirely new level of freedom

What that experience taught me is that when we listen to, accept, and embrace our sadness (or anger, frustration, boredom, etc.), we learn more about who we truly are and the types of limiting beliefs we may be living under. When I say "accept" and "embrace," I don't mean just give up or sit in a bad mood, allowing your mind to convince you of how terrible the world is. I mean totally change your perspective on your emotions and begin to appreciate and honor them as a guidance system that is leading you to a new, freer version of yourself. I mean letting the shell of your mind fall apart as you just sit with every ounce of pain it throws at you. Allowing yourself to fully experience every emotion that you feel is the gateway to actual transformation. There is no emotion, experience, or situation that is bigger than what you are. You are capable of growing beyond anything if you allow yourself to be with it.

When you cry, you release something. You've changed. You're lighter and suddenly you have a new perspective. Sometimes, right after we cry, we might even laugh. When we hold back our emotions and sweep them under the rug (often with Facebook, Netflix, and *Roseanne*) we put one more thing in the way of us and the flow of creativity and expression that wants to come through us in each and every moment. When we hold on to the trash bags that the generations before have handed us, we limit our ability to reach our true potential. We are meant to be constantly flowing and moving and changing, not to be these fearful stagnant beings that are only trying to protect themselves from fears that were passed down from their cashew-farming great-great-great-great-great-great-grandparents.

We are on the edge of evolution right now. We are transforming what it means to be alive. We're learning that the way we've played the game in the past no longer applies. We are change. We are love. We are sadness. We are all of it, and the moment that we embody that is the moment that we create true freedom, peace, and love in this world.

chapter 6

Remember Chapter Three?

I just have to take a second and talk about how good chapter three is. It's long, it's thorough, and it explains so many different things, while also being funny and delightful. I don't remember much of it, and I could easily go back and read it again, but all I know is that it's good. It's definitely in the top six chapters of this book so far.

Let's review all the different chapters that are in this book, in random order. There's four, two, *three*, one, five, and six. There are many different ways you could order these chapters. Another way you could look at them is six, five, *three*, one, two, four. No matter how you look at it, there are definitely six chapters. But three, three, baby, three is the gold. Three is the chapter that is so good that there's another chapter dedicated to its memory, chapter six, this chapter. Whenever you're on chapter six it makes you just think about the good old days when you were reading chapter three.

You might be thinking, "Is this chapter just here so Kyle can get closer to the sixty thousand words his publisher is asking for?" The answer is: nope, just really wanted to talk about how great chapter three is.

Now, it might seem weird, but I'd like to give a few reviews of chapter three. All these reviews are from me, but still, a review's a review. Again, these reviews will all contain words that definitely count toward that sixty-thousand-word total, however they in no way are specifically intended for that purpose.

> *"Chapter three, I can't believe I wrote chapter three."*
> —KYLE CEASE, AUTHOR

Kyle Cease says, *"You want to read a chapter? Check out three."*

> *"This is the third review of chapter three and I give chapter three three thrumbs thrup."*
> —KYLE CEASE, COMEDIAN

Kyle Cease also says, *"Also, chapter three is good, even my mom says so, and if you read chapter five, you know what a big deal that is for me."*

> *"Chapter three: it's not chapter ten."*
> —KYLE CEASE, PHILOSOPHER

Kyle Cease wants you to know: *"If you didn't understand chapter four, try reading chapter three; it's one less."*

Wow, it looks like people really loved chapter three. I can't wait to see what chapter the next chapter is about.

chapter 7

Show Up and Stay in the Room

I have to say, I'm absolutely in love with writing this book right now. It's really all I can think about. I never would have expected that, based on the six months of torture I put myself through before starting this, but now I can feel this process pulling me toward the highest version of myself that I have ever experienced, and it feels amazing. As I listen to the wisdom that has been coming through me into this book, I feel like I'm transforming into a completely different person. I seriously have zero desire to watch Netflix or go on Facebook right now. I would highly recommend the process of writing this book to anyone who has any addictions they want to let go of. Reading it is also an option.

There's a momentum that is happening now that is making this move faster and faster. At first, it took a lot of effort to even sit down and get to work because I didn't know if I could do it. If you picture digging an oil well, at first the only thing you can see is the dirt on top where you're starting. As you dig deeper and deeper, all you see is layers of dirt and mud; you don't even know if oil is actually there. You could be inches away from it, but for all you know you're miles away. Eventually, if you keep going, you'll strike oil, but up until that point you're moving entirely on faith. As I've continuously shown up and trusted that there is something in me that knows what it is doing, I'm now seeing results that I never could have envisioned before I started.

Parts of myself that were clinging to old stories have been falling away and there's a force that has taken over, driving me deeper into my oil well. The first couple chapters took like a week each to finish, not including those first six months, and now, the last few have taken just a day or two. I'm sure this process will start to get faster and faster and I'll probably end up writing a few chapters a day; maybe I'll even finish the entire thing today . . . in fact, maybe I have so much momentum that I'm already done and I don't even know it.

THE END

I just got off the phone with my publisher, Michele, and after a four-hour conversation, she explained to me that I'm not done, I've got way more to go. The conversation went like this:

INTERIOR: MICHELE's Office (Wide shot of a New York high-rise office)

MICHELE, a beautiful brunette who is one of the greatest publishers on the planet, debates whether or not fifteen thousand words is enough for KYLE's book.

Michele's phone: RINGTONE! (The ringtone is the Black
   Eyed Peas song "Where Is the Love?") MICHELE grace-
   fully pushes the "ignore" button.

Cut to: INTERIOR, apartment in Southern California

*KYLE, a very handsome top-model type, with expanding
biceps and ten-pack abs, handsomely pushes "redial" and calls
MICHELE back.*

*Cut to: MICHELE's phone. A brand-new iPhone 6 with a
beautiful case. A case that says the words "My owner is lenient
with word counts and will take a book with fifteen thousand to
maybe even twenty thousand words in it."*

*Michele's phone rings and plays the Black Eyed Peas again.
Michele gently pushes "accept."*

Michele

Hi, Kyle! Did you get your workout in today?

Kyle

Of course I did! Another day, another six hours at the gym!

Michele

Hahahaha! That's so true about days!

Kyle

I know, there are a lot of things true about days,

weeks, even years!

Michele

Kyle, the agreement was sixty thousand words. There is no way
out of this. You can't stop a book in the middle like that. I read
this thing about chapter six and then was shocked that the
book ended. I need you to actually finish the book.

Kyle

Oh, I totally know. I was just saying hi.

Michele

Oh, well, hi!

Kyle

Hi! What do you think of the book stopping around fifteen
thousand words?

Michele

I'm all for it.

Kyle

Okay, deal.

Michele

WAIT! I JUST REALIZED WHAT I SAID TO YOU!

Kyle

Too late. A deal is a deal.

Michele

I loved the Nickelback joke in chapter five. That was amazing.
You really must have worked on your deltoids. Seriously
though, the book has to have a middle and ending. This one
was just starting and that was it. All books I publish have
middles and endings. Also . . . I . . . beca—

Kyle

Wait, I actually couldn't hear the last part. I'm in a bad signal area.

Michele

What . . . Was . . . sa . . . I . . . cou . . .

Kyle

Yeah, see, I totally can't hear you now.

Michele

How about now?

Kyle

Oh yeah! I could hear that!

Michele

Okay, so what I wa . . . sa . . . thin . . . fitness . . . abs . . .
biceps . . . lower back more often.

Kyle

Yeah, you cut out again. It's so funny how I could hear you
when you asked if I could hear you but not when you said the
important stuff.

Michele

Ky . . . finish . . . the . . . whole . . . sixty thousand . . .
lawyers . . . prison . . . fraud . . . bottom of the ocean . . .
cement block . . . horse's head . . . frozen yogurt . . . Nancy
Grace . . .

Kyle

Yeah, I couldn't hear that.

Michele

How about now? Can you hear me now?

Kyle

(frustrated)

No, I will call you in a bit.

Michele

Late at night . . . stabbing . . . you . . . headless . . . book . . . or
else . . . dinner with friends . . . have to go . . . manicotti . . .
warming it up . . . guests . . . seven p.m. . . . let me know . . .

So it was a great call!

I guess I don't have as much momentum as I thought, but clearly this is getting easier and easier at an exponential rate. The reason that it's getting easier and easier is not that I'm getting better and better at writing; it's because I'm getting closer and closer to the calling that is pulling me forward. Every chapter I've written so far has revealed a new level of addiction that I've unconsciously been living in, and as I bring awareness to that part of myself, I move more into alignment with my intention. It's as if I'm unclogging the pipeline of limitless creativity that is feeding me these words. I'm starting to step out of the way as this book takes on a life of its own. It's beginning to feel more like this book is being written *through* me instead of *by* me. It's almost as if I am getting out of the way and it's writing itself.

It's honestly a little hard to believe. I started out totally against this and now it's the thing that is pulling me out of bed in the morning. It's almost like the scales have tilted and now my addiction has actually become writing the book. As I walk around during the day I'm just thinking about ways to make the book better and waiting until the moment I can get back home to work on it. Right now it would actually be harder for me to watch *Roseanne* than to write. If I tried, it would probably take me about six months to start and I'd have to figure out if I was going to watch *Roseanne* on my own or with a co-watcher. I'd then go to a cabin in Monterey to see if watching *Roseanne* would work better there. I'd be totally in my head about what my manager and my publisher thought about the episode of *Roseanne* I was watching and would constantly be second-guessing myself as I watched. (I'm not sure if you remember that earlier in the book, one of my addictions was watching *Roseanne*, but that's what I'm referring to. I switched how hard it was for me to start the book with how hard it would be to watch *Roseanne* now. Pretty good joke, huh?)

This is so unbelievably exciting to me because I'm getting the opportunity to experience and share, in real time, the type of transformation that I want to help others see is possible for them. I never thought that I could convey what I do onstage in a book, but in some ways it's turning out even better because of how much I've actually had to evolve in the process. I started out scared and not knowing what was going to happen, then as I started to break away from my past story, I felt sad because the part of myself that got love from other people was dying. Now that I'm on the other side of that sadness, excitement is taking over and pulling me toward a vision that's bigger than what I've seen before. These words are starting to pour out of me and there is literally no sense of my trying to push or control anything. Each sentence is unfolding on its own and leading me wherever I'm supposed to go. So maybe now I will let go *completely*.

Gorgonzola Greemelgritz said Grandpa Gravenstein had diarrhea with Grandma B in the produce section.

I think that sentence was an example of letting go a little too much. I should still make sure what I'm typing makes sense.

I'm starting to move into this place where fewer and fewer of my old beliefs, habits, and addictions are controlling me and more of my infinite creative possibility is taking over.

As you can see in the illustration below,
my creativity and artistic ability are at an all-time high.

Amount of Creativity Before   Amount of Creativity Now

And here's a pie graph for all the pie graph lovers.

My Creativity

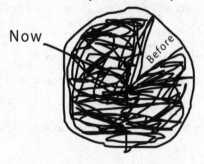

Now   Before

Based on the above graphic representations, it's now scientifically proven that I am in a creative flow and that the fears that I started this book with are almost completely gone. Nine out of ten dentists also agree that I am officially excited about this book and am moving deeper into the playful, childlike essence that is at my core. They also said I need to floss more. Then a new study debunked that

I need to floss more, so I stopped flossing. Now I get to have root canals! I have heard nothing but great things about those!

Even though those drawings are extremely well thought out and perfectly executed, I actually have another, non-joke-based graph that I like to use to show how we move from a fear-based, addictive, consumer mind-set into total creativity and freedom.

Here is the drawing that I'm talking about
(this description is probably unnecessary).

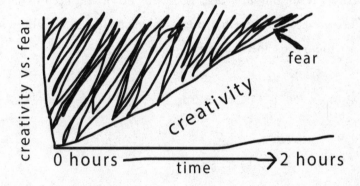

When we first start doing anything creative, the first couple minutes are hell. Our minds are in total fear of losing control to the creative part of ourselves. They're literally trying to save their lives and protect the stories they have created based on our pasts. Those first few minutes of torture are what we think it's going to be like the whole time, but as we stay in the room and just watch those fears as they come up, we create an opportunity for actual creativity to slip in. If we just keep going and don't let our minds pull us into some addiction or distraction, our hearts will begin to take over and guide us into that creative zone where we can tap into something truly unique and authentic. The more we do this, the more it becomes second nature for us and our entire lives become a reflection of being in that creative zone and being guided in every moment.

Staying in the room with my creativity is now keeping me in that zone all the time and, as a result, is causing me to effortlessly cut out the fat in my life: the addictions, the distractions, the people who don't bring out the highest in me. There's all sorts of stuff that we hold on to in our lives because we're scared of what will happen if we let it go, but all it does is slow us down and keep us small. When we let go of something that is taking up space in our lives, we make room for something else to come in.

Here's an illustration of the space we create when we let something go.

Space enlarged to show texture

As I've created the intention to live in my calling, it's almost like I've become a magnet for ideas and inspiration, where before I was a magnet for distractions. When we're in our head, the only thing we want is distractions that give us permission to stay in our head. When we're in our heart, we naturally move toward things that support our calling and internal evolution. This is what happens when you make your purpose more important than anything else. Instead of drifting aimlessly, your calling sets your course and pulls you into the actions needed to fulfill your purpose. When your intention beats habit, you win the game of life.

As I've stayed in this alignment, my heart is truly starting to open and I've gone from wanting my publisher to say I did a "good job" to feeling like there's something inside me that I *have* to share with the world. There is a message and a creative voice that has been dying to get out since I started this book, and now that the distractions and things that were blocking it are falling away, it's starting to fly onto the page.

Imagine what this could mean for you in *your* life . . . what intention is calling you into a completely new version of yourself? What would happen if you stepped out of the distractions around you and listened to the voice that wants you to share your gift with the world? You might go through a couple days of pain, but after that you'd feel a freedom that most dentists would agree could eliminate up to 99 percent of your addictions, which is the leading cause of gingivitis. (I meant that as a joke, but I bet there's some truth to that.)

Every single one of us has this calling within us, but most people are so locked into the habits and distractions they've created in their life that they can't hear it. It doesn't take anything special to discover what that calling is or what it wants you to do; all you have to do is turn down the volume of your distractions and listen. It takes maybe a day or two of stepping out of the addictions that keep you in a state of familiar complacency, and then you'll start to feel the pull of something bigger than you that wants to express itself through you.

There is something beyond us that wants to create on a level that we've never experienced before, not only for our benefit, but also for the benefit of the whole. The mind wants to keep you small and separate from the world. It pulls you into distraction after distraction, trying to keep you from the truth that what you are is just total love. The calling of our hearts is collaborative and has the ability to turn every situation into an opportunity for thriving. No matter what circumstances exist in your life, if you take even one step toward the calling of your heart, you'll begin to receive answers that you were blind to before. You'll grow beyond the problems and challenges that seem so overwhelming and start to see solutions that have been there the entire time.

I'm now in a place where I feel like I'm actually totally out of my head and being guided by my heart. I'm feeling connected to my purpose in this moment, which is calling me to share this message with the world and do everything I can to free people from the illusions they are living in. In this place, that feels so easy and inevitable. I know that the simple things that I'm doing, and not doing, on a daily basis are actually profound actions that are creating the foundation and internal alignment that are allowing me to write these words faster and more effectively. As I'm clearing out the things that have been blocking my calling from coming through, I feel like I'm holding on to a giant balloon that is lifting me out of my old story.

When I stay in my calling and grab on to that balloon, I can feel my perspective raise and any problems that I might have been dealing with aren't even there anymore. What I mean by that is, when we're holding on to the limitations that are familiar and "safe," they keep us at the same level of awareness we've always been at. When we let go of those beliefs, maybe by taking an action that was scary to us before, we're actually entering into an entirely new dimension where we transcend our old challenges and create a whole new set of opportunities for ourselves. If we stop believing the lies our minds tell us about what is and isn't possible in our lives, we can untie ourselves from those beliefs and allow our balloons to naturally rise.

Once we have untied ourselves from the distractions, addictions, and limiting beliefs that keep us stuck on the ground, we'll begin to notice the billions of ideas and opportunities out there just waiting for someone to step up and grab them. The idea to create the lightbulb was always there, just waiting for someone to catch it. Thankfully, Abraham Lincoln had raised his alignment enough so that he could see it, otherwise we'd all be reading this in the dark. To end this chapter I'd like to share a famous quote of his:

I have a dream: the Gettysburg Address.
—ABRAHAM LINCOLN, INVENTOR OF THE LIGHTBULB

chapter 8

Why People's Opinions of You Aren't Real

If you're reading this right now, then congratulations, you've officially made it further into a book than I ever have. I guess there's also a chance that you're *not* reading this right now and that you gave up around chapter five. If that's the case, it's too bad, because it was just starting to get good. I realize you may never read this, person who stopped at chapter five, but I just want to say I still love you, even though you probably stopped right before this book was about to change your life. Maybe someday you'll stumble on this book while cleaning out your attic and, as our eyes meet again after what might seem like a lifetime apart, that spark will still be there and we'll pick up right where we left off. Although, now that I think about it, where the hell have you been? Seriously, all you had to do was read for a couple more hours and you would have had this book finished a long time ago. I'm not sure if I even want to be read by you anymore.

That got weird. I'm not sure what happened there. I think maybe I've had too many girlfriends who have made me watch *The Notebook* with them. For the rest of you who *are* reading this right now, I apologize for that last paragraph, or lastagraph (saving time [I've discovered that you really can save a lot of time if you combine words, or cords (combine words [I realize now we're not actually saving any time (I could have just ended at "last paragraph" but now I'm basically writing an entire new paragraph just explaining this [this is just to prove to you I can make a sixth parenthesis (so, to review: I apologize for making the last thing way too long [apololong (ninth parenthesis)])])])]). Just to make sure we're all on the same page though, here's a simple and helpful graphic to help you decide what to do next:

how long has it been since you last read this book?

a year or more

a few months

i've been reading straight through

seriously? what have you been doing?

ok, a little inconsistent, but not bad. what have you been doing?

great job!

saving babies   yelling at babies

in your free time, would you rather...

oh, good job. but you should go back to the beginning because there is no way you remember it.

saving babies   yelling at babies

save babies   yell at babies

awesome, time well spent. i'd suggest maybe just rereading the last chapter so you can get back up to speed. all in all though, great job.

congratulations, you are the best type of person reading this book. keep reading.

go back to the beginning because there is no way you remember it. and stop yelling at babies, try saving babies instead.

that's not a good excuse. in fact, it's the worst excuse. go back two chapters so you can get back up to speed. try saving babies instead.

me too. keep reading.

So far, you've seen me scared, you've seen me have all the answers, you've seen me feeling sad, and you've seen me excited and playful. You've seen me be totally in my head and freaking out and you've seen me transcend those fears and move into my heart, and hopefully you've been moving more into your heart too. I've been an insane tornado of emotions on the surface. I've had to experience all those emotions fully and allow them to move through me so that I can connect to the deepest part of myself, which is actually the space where all of those emotions arise. This chapter's going to be cool.

I'm still feeling emotions, and I'm still hearing the thoughts that my head is throwing at me, but now I'm feeling more connected to the space that those thoughts and emotions are in. It's almost as if I'm standing outside of myself and just watching as feelings and thoughts come and go, without the need to act on every impulse.

One of the most basic illusions that we are under is that we believe we *are* whatever we are experiencing. I am sad. I am happy. I am poor. I am sick. I am young. Those things aren't what you are, they are just circumstances on the surface of your life. What you actually are is beyond all of that. You are the sky, not just the clouds. You are the ocean, not just the waves. You are Disneyland, not just Space Mountain. You are the Beatles' entire catalog, not just "Can't Buy Me Love." You are the entire cast of *Roseanne*, not just Jackie. Some of those metaphors are better than others, but you're the paragraph, not just the metaphor. This is probably starting to not make sense, but you're the making, not just the sense. I don't know what I'm doing right now with all these stupid metaphors, but I'm the doing, not just all these stupid metaphors.

This is a pretty big concept that can be hard to grasp—that's probably why I used so many metaphors that were hard to grasp. Actually, the mind can't ever truly grasp this; it can only be felt by the heart. It might be easy for some people to understand intellec-tually, but it's another thing to actually experience and know it. My challenge here is that I don't just want to describe something that I've experienced to you. I want to connect and write from a place of knowing that we are more than just the emotions, thoughts, stories, beliefs, possessions, grandmas, and situations in our lives so that these words can awaken that same space in you. I guess it might still help to tell you the story of how I woke up to that space in me.

When I was ten years old, I had the chance to visit a chocolate factory that had been closed down for several years but somehow still managed to produce the world's most delicious sweets. The reclusive owner had offered a tour of the factory and a lifetime sup-ply of chocolate to anyone who could find one of his magical golden tickets, and for some reason, when he announced that, the entire world went apeshit . . . wait, that's the plot of *Willy Wonka and the Chocolate Factory*. I always get that movie and my life mixed up.

Here's the real story . . .

Back when I was Gene Wilder . . . hold on.

Okay, the real story is, I ended up on a boat that suddenly made the whole movie so surreal and caused all the kids who watched it to have nightmares. I'm thrown off again, I'm sorry.

Seriously though, here's the story: My parents are Oompa-Loompas and my brother is made out of chocolate. This is also wrong. Now I am just combining *Willy Wonka* with real life.

HERE WE GO.

When I was first starting to have some success as an actor and comedian, I believed that I was what I achieved. I was completely lost in the story of what I did for a living. I got a lot of love and attention for it, so on a shallow level it was an easy story to buy into. There was a time when I wasn't willing to go to a party unless the people there knew "who I was" and what I had done. I wore the false story of who I thought I was as a shield. We almost all do this in our own way. Many people think who they are is who they're dating or what their body looks like or the amount of money that they have. Wayne Dyer once said, "When the thing that you think you are goes away, then you go away too." That might not be exactly how he said it; it was probably more poetic and smarter sounding than that.

Because I was so involved in the story of what I achieved, I was constantly striving to do and get more to keep that story alive. If things were going well, I'd be happy, at least on a surface level (which, at the time, was the highest level of happiness I knew about). After a while though, I realized that it took bigger and bigger things to keep that story going, and even after accomplishing something massive, I'd feel great for a little while, but within hours or even minutes I'd think, "What's next?"

At a certain point, my story began to sabotage me and I developed a crippling anxiety that made it hard for me to even stand. I started to create a belief that I might faint onstage. I eventually overcame that anxiety by realizing how powerful my thoughts were and learning how to take control of them. I got really excited to share this information with other people and ended up creating a workshop for aspiring comedians on how to get into a creative flow state onstage. As soon as I created that, I started to hear that some people I knew were talking crap about me, saying how I had gone crazy and started a cult or something.

One thing I've learned from this is that any time you do something positive or different from the masses, some people will think you're in a cult. Well, they might not automatically assume you're in a cult, but the point is, when we do something out of the norm we're often met with resistance from people in our lives who don't want us to change. Many times people get scared when someone close to them changes or does something different because they are afraid to change themselves. As a society, we're so used to the judgment and negativity of the world that anything outside of those boundaries can actually feel threatening to the way of life that has become comfortable to us.

You: It's so nice outside.
Your friend: What are you, a Scientologist or something?
You: I'll just shut up.

For the record, I don't have anything against Scientologists. I don't really know a lot about them; they're probably nice people. I wasn't great at science in high school, and I don't think they even offered tologist classes where I lived, so it probably just not for me.

So anyway, I started this workshop and I really loved doing it because I was able to speak from my heart and talk about comedy too. It was my first taste of what I get to do now, bridging comedy and transformation. I was starting to realize that there was something beyond just trying to build up my story so that people would like me and was getting really inspired by helping people move past their fears and into more creativity. Hearing that people were talking behind my back still bothered me though, and at one point I actually said to Louie Anderson, whom I was working with at the time, "I really want to get over what people think of me."

What happened an hour later is really crazy because it's almost like someone heard me say that and decided to make me face it head-on. I was in a hotel getting ready to leave when someone sent me an email with a subject line that said, "Hey, you con man." The email said that he had just read a blog that another famous comedian had written about me, and he sent me the link to it. I clicked the link and it led me to the blog, which said that the workshop I had created was a total scam and that I was a fraud and all of these insanely hurtful things. It was written by a comic, so not only were the things he said really mean, but they were also really well written, convincing, and actually pretty funny. Even I started to not like me.

This was one of my peers. I cared a lot about what people thought about me, but as a comic, I *really* cared what other comics thought of me. It was fascinating how someone who wasn't there had interpreted what that workshop was about and what my motives were. I might have written it off as just someone else's misinformed opinion, but when I looked at the bottom of the blog, I could see it was going viral and being shared thousands of times by tons of other comics and fans.

In that moment, my ego went crazy. Blood rushed to my head and my heart started racing. I was having a full-on panic attack. The story that I had been working on my entire life was falling apart. I had the craziest, most depressing thoughts about how this was the end of my career and how I was going to lose all my friends. A car was waiting for me outside, but I told the driver to just leave without me. This was so big that I needed to sit and feel it for a while.

At this point, I knew enough not to numb the pain and get addicted to something. It would have been really easy for me to drain the minibar and separate myself from what was happening, but I at least knew that there was something I needed to learn here. I literally sat, by myself, for several days in a hotel room just letting my mind go crazy.

My mind was coming up with all of these ways that I was going to *achieve* my way out of it. I thought if I got another Comedy Central special and just totally nailed it, then I would prove everyone wrong and I could repair my story. I was coming up with the craziest, most elaborate plans for how I was going to overcome this. The real problem was that I had a belief there was actually something to overcome.

At a certain point, I started noticing that I was just in an argument with myself.

My mind: How am I going to fix this?

My mind: Why even try, it's all over. I'm so sad it's over.

My mind: I'm so pissed right now, I feel like punching something.

My mind: What if I land a huge role in a movie? That'll show everyone.

My mind: Yeah, but I won't get cast in any movies, not after this.

My mind: What would be a good thing to punch?

My mind: If I have an amazing gig, that would fix everything.

My mind: Why don't you just punch your own face, you stupid idiot?

My mind: Yeah, I'll punch my own face, that'll show everyone.

My mind was in a perpetual state of creating a problem, fixing it, and then breaking it again. The mind loves to come up with its own problem and then solve the problem that it just created. It's actually how it creates the illusion that it's in control.

My mind became so ridiculously chaotic that it just started to turn into this weird character that I was watching. I was sitting on a bed in an air-conditioned hotel room, totally safe, but inside, my mind was destroying itself. Eventually, the insanity of my mind became so outrageous that I couldn't help but realize it was all a lie. Everything I was protecting, fixing, and mourning was just imaginary bullshit. Then, all of a sudden, it almost felt like my mind moved outside of my head and I saw it as separate from me. I became aware that my mind wasn't me, it was some other entity on autopilot trying to save its life as it crash-landed into itself. In the moment that I had that awareness, I could feel everything just drop. The argument, the anger, the sadness, and my entire past story totally dissolved, and a space between me and my thoughts opened up. It felt as if I had been unknowingly carrying this hundred-pound weight my entire life, and in that instant, I finally got to let it go. All those voices stopped and I remember feeling how present I was in the moment. I spent the next few hours just staring at the wall feeling total bliss.

When I started noticing that those voices weren't me, that they were just thoughts happening inside of me, I started to identify more with the awareness of who I *am* than the mind's story of *who I think I am*. I actually noticed that the voices in my head were separate from the part of me watching them. I realized that I was totally safe and the voices were the cause of the chaos. I moved beyond the mind and into the space that watches the mind. It's freaky, I know.

I spent the entire next day feeling absolutely incredible, peaceful, and in such appreciation for life. I had moved beyond the running narrative of my mind and into the pure awareness that is at the core of my existence. I was totally present with every person I met and felt such a connection to myself and others. The filter that was standing between me and everything I experienced was gone and life looked totally different.

The next day I flew home and wanted to watch a movie, but every DVD I put in wouldn't work. I tried like five or six different ones and then finally, the one that worked was a movie called *Adaptation*. At one point in the movie I heard a line that changed my life and confirmed everything I was discovering in my own experience. In one of the scenes, Nicolas Cage says something like this to his twin brother (who happens to also be played by Nicolas Cage, which was a good casting decision), "In high school there was a girl that you loved who was making fun of you, but you didn't care. Why?" and his brother says, "It was mine, that love. Even Sarah didn't have the right to take it away. I can love whoever I want." Then he said the line that changed my life: "You are what you love, not what loves you."

In this new awareness that I had discovered, I had the depth to understand what that truly meant. When I was in a place of being "what loves me," I was a slave to the person or thing I wanted. If my motive is to get something from someone, I'm sacrificing myself and doing everything I can to make sure that person will like me so I can get what I want. If I move from a place of "I am what I love," I can go back to that effortless childhood place of what I actually am, which is total inner freedom, and I can transcend all of the stories I have about myself. Those stories don't exist.

When you were a kid you just did what you loved to do, no matter what anyone else thought of you. In that place, it doesn't matter what someone else's opinion of you is; you have something deeper that is moving you. That level of freedom is still available to all of us if we go back to doing what we love just because WE LOVE IT, not because we think we can GET LOVE from someone outside of ourselves.

As I heard the line from *Adaptation*, I got the answer to the question of how to get over what people think of me. I realized that what people think of me isn't even real. The only thing that makes their opinion of me real is if I'm more focused on what *I think* they're thinking of me than *the calling of my heart*. You probably had to read that sentence twice. I tried making it easier to understand with the italic thing, but that was the best I could do. Basically, you only care about what someone else thinks about you when you're in your head, because that's the only place an opinion exists. When you're in your heart, you're just creativity, love, and effortless expression. What people think about what you're doing doesn't even register.

I flew to a gig in Florida a few days later, still feeling amazing and without an ounce of nerves. As I walked onstage I was totally present with everyone that I interacted with, and when they handed me the microphone it was just another moment, no different from the rest. I was in such a state of connection to myself that a whole new me came through that was more playful and creative than I had ever been before, and tons of brand-new material unfolded effortlessly. The crowd went crazy and I walked offstage as they gave me a standing ovation, but I didn't even care or notice really (although, I guess I did notice because I just told you about it). It was probably the best performance I've ever had. In that moment the blog that comic had written and other people's opinions had no effect on me—in fact, they didn't even exist in my reality.

Over time, that feeling of total freedom from the story of myself faded a bit, and the gravitational pull of my identity sucked me back in to some degree, but that experience showed me something that I can't unsee. It showed me how lost we are in the stories of our lives and how those stories are really just a lie. I was totally trapped in the belief that I had to protect the story of who I was, and as soon as I stepped out of that belief I experienced true freedom for the first time.

Any pain that we ever experience is really just because of a thought that we've decided to believe. The belief that my career was going to be over was just a thought that I created out of thin air. We choose to believe all sorts of things that cause us pain. I currently have a belief that I'll probably never get to marry Jennifer Aniston. That causes me a great deal of pain. But the truth is, I don't know if that's actually true. I don't know for sure that she won't see me somewhere and think that my deep insight and comedic wit would be a perfect match for her striking good looks and attractive personality. I don't know if it's true that we won't have our first date at a bowling alley and she won't be so impressed at how amazing I am at bowling that she'll instantly fall in love with me. I don't know that the media won't start calling us "Kylefer" or that we won't end up having a family that harmonizes together like a modern-day Partridge Family. I have no way of knowing that won't happen.

Really though, I'm not in pain because I believe I won't get to marry Jennifer Aniston. I'm in pain because I have a belief that I need Jennifer Aniston to be happy. My problem is just that I'm in resistance to the thought that I might not be with Jennifer Aniston. In other words, I'm arguing with *what is*. I'm believing that who I am is what Jennifer Aniston thinks about me. If I realize that *I just love Jennifer Aniston*, then it doesn't matter if we get married or if I even meet her. My happiness and fulfillment are based on my love going outward, not what comes back to me. True happiness comes from sharing love, not from getting love. Also, the Jennifer Aniston thing is mostly a joke. The truth is I have a small, non-stalkery-type crush on her and I'm not really in pain because I'm not with her . . . it was just a good example. Although, I'm open to the possibility of "Kylefer" if you are, Jennifer Aniston.

This isn't a belief for me, it's a knowing and embodied fact: our happiness is not in anything external. Nobody and nothing has control of your happiness. If you think you need something for you to be happy, you make that thing your god. When you realize that the belief that you need any circumstance to be a certain way for you to be happy is a lie, you are totally free. You can't get more happy because of any external thing. I'm not saying that you can't enjoy external things—you absolutely can, and I do—but every time you try to get *love* from an external source you cut off the love that you already are. You are naturally happy in the absence of the belief that you need something outside of yourself to get happy. I've learned that it's not "When something happens, I'll be happy," it's "When I'm happy, things will happen."

When you live in this place of natural self-connection, the side benefit is that you become totally creative and insightful, and things start to happen *for* you. You become a magnet for other circumstances and relationships that reflect the happiness that you have inside. You start to attract thoughts and ideas that access new opportunities that will match your level of alignment. When I went onstage after realizing all of this, there was a new flow of inspiration coming through that allowed me to create at a higher level than I ever had before. If I'm connected to the happiness within myself that isn't dependent on anything, then I can go onstage and not be a victim of the opinions of my audience. It allows my most authentic self to come through and create an actual relationship with their hearts. Instead of presenting some manipulation to get something from them, I *give* all of myself to them, and as a by-product receive even more.

The beliefs "I am not enough," "My happiness is outside of me," and "I don't deserve love" are just illusions that block us from our true happiness. These kinds of beliefs are at the core of our identities and can be hard to see beyond because we think these beliefs are *who we are*. Letting go of a belief like that can be as scary as letting go of a limb, but if you've ever believed something about yourself and then later that belief changed, then there is no way that what you are is your beliefs, because your belief changed and you still existed.

What I've discovered over years of inner exploration is that nothing I believe about myself is actually true. It's always changing and shifting . . . and especially now that I know this, my beliefs seem to change every couple of minutes. Sometimes I really believe that long-term relationships aren't for me, and then the next day I tell all my friends about the soul mate I just met. In fact, as soon as you finish this book you should pick up my next book, titled *Why My Last Book Was Wrong*. That's mostly a joke. The things I'm talking about in this book aren't really beliefs. They are feelings and insights that are coming up in the moment as I stay present and listen to my heart. I'm not saying everything in this book is right for everyone all the time, but I can say everything I've said in this book was true for me at the time that I wrote it, with the level of awareness that I had at the time. That's really the best anyone can say about anything they share.

So if you're not your beliefs, then what exactly are you? You're not your body, because you were in one body when you were five and you're in a completely different body now (unless you are a five-year-old, in which case I can't believe you made it this far, you're probably the next Buddha. I'm sorry for the adult language). You know you can't be your emotions, because you're probably in a different mood now than you were just a few hours ago, even though when we're in pain, we often convince ourselves we're going to feel that way forever.

It's easy for us to know that we're not any of our five senses because those are constantly changing. We're always seeing, smelling, tasting, hearing, and feeling something different. We never taste a cheeseburger and think, "I am a cheeseburger." If you know you're not what you taste because what you're tasting always changes, why would you think that you are what you believe if that changes too?

Other than the fact that I'm experiencing all of these things—my emotions, my thoughts, my body, my senses—I still don't *fully* know what I am. Thank god I don't know, because now I get to be on a constant journey of discovering what I am by uncovering more and more of what I'm not and letting go of it. I get to become the space that all of this moves through and continuously evolve into an even bigger and freer space that can experience deeper and richer aspects of life. I get to embrace the darkness and pain within myself because I know that's not me. I get to give love to the limited story I created as a child. I get to move beyond the differences between myself and others because I know those differences are illusions. When we can see the space beyond the skin color, the story, and the beliefs, we'll finally realize that we are actually connected in a way we never fully understood before. Let's explore that now.

chapter 9

Uninformative Chapter Title

That chapter title might be confusing . . . I'm not really saying that this chapter is uninformative, I'm saying that this chapter has a title that is uninformative; the chapter itself is actually very informative. Although, don't confuse this chapter with chapter ten, which is titled "The Very Informative Chapter." Strangely, that chapter is actually extremely *uninformative*. It's basically just a picture of a baby inside of a taco. Feel free to flip to that chapter now to confirm that.

See, it's just a baby in a taco, no information at all. Basically, what happened was, I came up with that joke in the previous paragraph and then made the chapter with a picture of a baby in a taco as a by-product. I found out later that if you stare at a picture of a baby in a taco long enough, you will become enlightened. For most people it takes five to six hours, but if you have a stressful job it could be a little longer. If you haven't forgiven your parents yet, it could be up to a week. If you're a politician, a baby in a taco won't work. You need a baby in a burrito. Stare at this baby in a burrito for a month:

So, as I said before, after having this huge internal shift as a result of being called out by those other comics, I saw something new and was now being called into a deeper level of purpose and alignment. I realized that almost all of my fears were an illusion and I caught a glimpse of what life is like when I'm able to see beyond the story of who I think I am. The only thing I could think about after that was how to stay in that effortless place of knowing and trusting that everything is taken care of. I now had to match that level of inner awareness with my external actions. Once I experienced this new world, there was no going back.

It's like if you were someone who spent your entire life weighing five hundred pounds and then you somehow experienced what life would be like weighing a hundred and fifty pounds—the only thing you would care about is finding a way to get back to the experience of weighing a hundred and fifty pounds. Even though the experience of being a hundred fifty pounds was there the entire time, once you felt it and knew that it was actually real and possible, you'd have much more of an incentive to move toward it. That experience would be even more powerful than all the cheeseburgers and pizza that would usually tempt you into staying five hundred pounds.

I started moving from the phase of making it happen and achieving into the phase of letting go of my limited story and tapping into some part of myself that seemed to be beyond my external accomplishments. I had experienced what it was like to feel totally free and complete, and I realized that I don't actually need anything outside of myself to feel that. In fact, I realized that many of the things I was holding on to in my life were actually the things that were blocking me from accessing that feeling that is always within me.

Even though this isn't necessarily the way that I see life now, at that moment, the next step that I had to take was to learn how to let go of everything that was in the way of being in that space of infinite possibility. I realized that there were layers and layers of habits and addictions in my life that were keeping me away from that feeling of unlimited joy. I was in a completely new realm where instead of trying to pile on achievements and material possessions, I was on a mission to release myself from needing any of that stuff.

It's almost like if you were in a dark room and all of a sudden you saw this horrific car crash right in front of you. You'd immediately rush to try to help those people or call 911, but if you were to suddenly realize that you were actually in a movie theater and what you were watching was just film projected onto a screen, you wouldn't need to do anything about the crash; it'd just be an illusion.

So the goals in my life suddenly switched from fixing what was happening on the screen to figuring out how to leave the movie theater and move past the story of my old life. The most important part of that had already happened: realizing that I was in a movie theater. The next part was even harder though; I now had to pull myself away from the illusions being projected on the screen that I had learned to become addictively obsessed with.

I started to think, "What is in the way of me finding myself?" I already knew that one of the biggest addictions I had in my life was food, so I decided the first thing I was going to do was let go of eating addictively. Food, and the health of my body, was something that had been a challenge for me almost my entire life. As a child, I learned to equate eating with connecting to the people around me. I loved going out to dinner with my mom and family, and I remember eating out at restaurants as being some of the only times that I was able to get my dad's undivided attention. As an adult, I found myself eating whatever my friends and people around me wanted to eat, instead of what my body actually wanted. I was so lost in going with the flow of other people's desires that I didn't even actually know what my body was truly asking for. I'm pretty sure it wasn't Doritos though. I'll probably get an angry letter from Doritos now. I wonder if all the angry letters that Doritos sends out have nacho cheese fingerprints on them. Now I kind of hope I do get a letter from them. Seriously though, something that I do know from the depths of my heart is that the letter would be coming from their attorney and it would probably be via email or just really good stationery, and it's really doubtful that there would be nacho cheese fingerprints on it. I know in my soul that the attorney would have the awareness to wash his hands after eating Doritos, and just because the attorney works for Doritos, it doesn't mean he eats more Doritos than other people. He's just their attorney.

So I decided to start off by declaring to my friends, family, and following that I was going to spend the next ninety days eating only raw vegan food. It's funny how extreme it seemed at the time to not eat any cooked, processed, or animal-based food. That's what the majority of animals on this planet eat instinctually. I don't know why it's more normal for us to eat food that has been chemically engineered, cooked, and processed than food that grows naturally, but that's not the point. I'm not trying to get you to be vegan; don't freak out.

From where I was, this was a huge leap. I was going to eat only healthy, raw food for ninety days straight. I was making this commitment for a bigger reason than to just change my body; I was doing this to rewrite and transcend my beliefs about myself. To make sure that I stuck to it, I pledged to give away $10,000 if I ate anything cooked or anything unhealthy. One thing that I had learned from the motivational speaker Tony Robbins was to get on the island and burn the boats. Creating that insane goal and consequence pushed me to actually do it. This way, any time I saw a cookie, I knew it would turn into a $10,000 cookie if I ate it.

So I started my journey of ninety days eating only raw vegan. In the first two weeks, it was crazy how much my ego and my emotions were craving crappy food. I could feel my old story breaking apart. I could feel how every time I was sad, I wanted to eat the kind of food that I ate as a kid when I was hanging out with my mom. So it wasn't even my body that was hungry, it was my emotions. I could feel how much I really wanted to eat at Taco Time or places that my family used to go to. Taco Time is a restaurant in Seattle that I love, mainly out of nostalgia, but my buddy Dan hates it. That surprises me, because all I've known for my entire life is that Taco Time is the best restaurant in the world, but maybe it's possible that I just associate Taco Time with my mom, so it tastes better to me than Dan. He says they just serve mayonnaise tacos.

If Taco Time feels the urge to send some guys to talk to him, his current address is 26734 Juniper Lane, Apartment 3B, Sherman Oaks, CA 92742. Go to the gate and ring the button to apartment 3B and say the secret code word, "Baconator," to the guard, and they'll let you in. Or at least Taco Time could have their attorneys send Dan a letter. Dan would probably think the stains on his letter are from mayonnaise, but I would know that the stains are actually from a homemade, delicious, creamy ranch-style dressing that is the perfect complement to an authentic Mexican taco, burrito, or chimichanga. Dan would think it's mayonnaise because he doesn't understand the hard work that Taco Time puts into their food, and their letters. I would bet that even their *letters* use the freshest ingredients. I am so damn hungry right now.

As I continued my ninety days, I would sense and feel that my body was getting gradually more and more healthy. I also started to discover a connection to myself that trumped my desire for attention and external connection. It was becoming easier and easier to say no to doing things that weren't my highest calling, and eventually, I felt no guilt or fear if I told my friends that I would not go out and eat an unhealthy meal with them. I was starting to actually make myself a priority. My calling was starting to win over *everything*.

I know that deep down my body didn't want to eat cheese sticks or pizza; it was never asking for that, but my emotions were. I noticed my body was constantly getting more and more excited about what this could mean, while my mind was experiencing a combination of pain as I let go and absolute fulfillment as I started to discover for the first time that I could change my habits.

At one point around a month in, I noticed that when I smelled cooked food, it started to smell more like chemicals and metal than something that I actually wanted to eat. It was almost like I was now detached from an old story where I thought that I needed to eat certain things to get love. I was aware that I could go for at least a month eating nothing but raw organic food. My body started to change its habits to only wanting healthy organic food. I was becoming more and more free. I just needed to let go of what felt heavy and my body would know how to take over.

I had been so conditioned to think that I needed to eat certain things every day, and I was freeing myself from that conditioning as I just ate what my body wanted and stopped carrying the weight of my old story around. Now that I was coming from a purer, cleaner place that could identify the gross heaviness of the food that I had been eating, I started thinking, "What else in my life feels gross and heavy?" My internal awareness was growing and my standards for what I would accept in my body and my life were higher, so I started letting go of other things too. I stopped being on Facebook. I stopped hanging around with people who didn't support me. I even stopped dating for a while. As I kept letting go of things, I was getting closer to the core of myself. I kept cleaning out all of these old addictions and was left with just me. I was letting go of everything I was not, to make room for the birth of what I actually am.

At times I would feel sad as I let go of a familiar story, but because I had begun to understand that all sadness is just a passing thing, I would actually choose to walk into that sadness, let go of whatever I needed to let go of, and just let myself feel everything I was experiencing. My awareness had taught me to just hold on and walk right into the storm because on the other side of that sadness was an entirely new me. I would get closer and closer to the truth of what I was by choosing to stay in the room with my intention to grow and not necessarily attach to whatever was falling off of me. I just grabbed on to my new intention to expand and stay with the moment as I allowed the old story to peel off. I even started understanding that if I am feeling really sad and lost, I should get excited, because it means I'm about to discover a new level of freedom, love, and expansion that I've never ever experienced in my entire life.

Throughout this ninety-day process, I was constantly surprised by how as soon as I would go through the pain of letting go of something, I would feel the joy and freedom that I'd thought I would get through that thing I was holding on to or chasing.

It was like not breathing the air that's in front of you because you think that someone or something else has the air you need, but there's air right in front of your face; it's all around you all the time. If you replace oxygen with love, you realize all you have to do is breathe to feel the love that you already are.

It's one thing to know this intellectually, but to actually get rid of those things so that you *have* to breathe your own air is a whole different world.

At one point, my entire journey became about letting go of anything that felt heavy to me. I started to notice that I could easily make decisions based on whether something felt heavy or light in my body. Any time you think of something, there is an instinctual feeling that you have in your entire body that will tell you all that you need to know. Right after you have that feeling, you'll feel your mind kick in and start to justify why you should keep or hold on to that thing, but if you just listen to that first instinct, you'll start to make decisions that are in alignment with your soul and your natural guidance. I started to get excited about following that instinctual, gut-level feeling in every situation, even if it seemed crazy and I couldn't see any external evidence for why I should do it.

Probably six weeks in, as I was listening more and more to my heart, I realized that it was no longer my highest calling to perform as a stand-up comic. Even though my comedy career was at an all-time high, it didn't feel fulfilling anymore. It was exciting, it made me good money, it was my dream career, but there was something in me that said: "I don't think that my highest fulfillment is going on tour performing for people in comedy clubs anymore. Even though I don't know what it is, there's something in me that's bigger. Even though I don't know the specifics of it, I somehow know there's something that is so much more fulfilling and will change the world and help me to grow in a much more powerful way."

So, even though I had all of this abundance in this absolute dream career, I decided to quit cold turkey. I pulled out a video camera and said, "I'm officially done doing comedy clubs on the road." Right when I said that, three auditions showed up in my phone. I'm not making any claim here, but it almost felt like I made room for those auditions to show up. In a practical sense, I actually did make room for them, because otherwise I would have been on the road and wouldn't have been able to take them.

We can't ever allow something new to come into our lives until we make room for it. Many times we'll be in relationships that are unfulfilling, wishing that we were in better relationships, but we don't let go of the relationships we're in because we're afraid we won't actually find better ones. We're waiting for a sure thing to show up before we let go of what we don't want, so we stay in the alignment of the relationships we don't want and they end up being all we can attract. We've got one foot in the past while the other foot is trying to move toward something new, but we end up in this kind of limbo where we're just stuck and not making progress in either direction. It's amazing how much we hold on to things we don't want out of the fear of losing them.

Deciding to quit doing comedy clubs on the road was a very scary declaration, but I trusted that calling inside me and let go of it. At first, I went through a period of sadness because of the obvious, surface-level things I was missing out on, and then I realized, "Wow, I'm moving completely based on faith. I'm making decisions from just what I'm feeling in my body without any physical evidence of why I should do this. I'm making decisions from my heart." It felt like throwing away a broken compass and picking up a brand-new digital GPS system. It wasn't like the GPS I have in my car, which makes me feel like I'm doing everything wrong. The GPS I got had a normal, pleasant woman's voice that didn't sound like she was angry with me.

It was almost as if I was starting to train myself to cocreate with the universe. It was telling me a feeling and I knew that all I had to do was honor that feeling and move on faith. So I did. That faith was tested a ton because I was getting calls and offers for gigs on the road all the time, and I said no to them. I felt myself get more into alignment with myself as I realized, "I'm a guy who can say no to that level of temptation. I'm even more powerful than the high-paying gigs that are coming in. I'm even bigger than my childhood dream career." As I said no to the highest version of my story that I had ever known, I was creating space to grow even bigger and learning to make decisions based off of *me and myself* versus *me and my circumstances*.

So I just kept honoring the feelings that were coming through, and even though I said good-bye to that career and felt sadness and fear and insecure moments, I also felt a deep fulfillment as I honored the calling in my body and kept saying yes to the feeling. I felt myself connecting to myself again. We rarely connect to ourselves. We never listen to what we actually want, and because we are confused about what we want, life gives us back the confusion we've unconsciously requested. We do what we think we *should* do and we don't honor what our bodies say they *want* to do. This calling is in us all day telling us what to do, and we've trained ourselves to ignore it and just be this giant collection of whatever everyone else tells us we should do as we keep ignoring that feeling. When we actually tune into that deep wisdom that knows what to do, it feels awkward and scary at first, but eventually we get a momentum that overrides our old habits and addictions.

Once I had said no enough times, I stepped into the realization that I'm even more incredible than the story of this huge comedy career. I'm not saying this from a place of bragging about myself, I'm saying this because I want everyone to know that they are even more incredible than they understand, and if they stay in a place of listening to what that calling wants, they will experience that for themselves.

Actually taking these leaps without seeing where I would land was creating a new excitement and confidence in me that was making me feel unstoppable and creating a space for even bigger ideas and visions for the future. All of a sudden I heard this feeling come in and it said, "Combine comedy and transformation." It said, "What you're learning right now, it's your job to communicate that to the public and make it funny." When I thought that, I didn't know the specifics and I didn't know what it would look like, but I did know that on some level it made sense to me. Because I was in a place of alignment with myself that understood my inner guidance was always right and all I had to do was honor it, I didn't question it. The part of me that was still scared said, "But nobody's ever done that before," and then my soul said, "Exactly, no one's ever done that before!"

So I realized my job is to do this new, scary, unpredictable thing because it's original, it's exciting, and it's something that is actually the most effortless option in the long run. It's in the highest demand of what would help the world. It's so powerful and it's the most fulfilling thing I can do. It's a win-win-win. It helps me, it helps other people, and it helps the world.

I decided, "Okay, I don't know how, but I'm going to combine comedy and transformation." As I opened up to that possibility, an entirely new level of inspiration came through and ideas were coming in from every angle about how I could do that. One thought that grabbed me was the idea of doing the lecture circuit at colleges. I had performed at many colleges as a comedian and now I thought maybe what I would do is figure out how to combine comedy and transformation and speak at different colleges. I started making videos with my friend Diego for the bookers of almost every college that I had performed at by name. We sat down and for a week or two, made video after video, and I would look into the camera and say: "Hi, this video is for Diane Johnson of North Idaho University. My name is Kyle Cease and I've performed at your college as a stand-up comic. Well, I'd like to talk to you about doing the lecture circuit at your college and making it funny. I want to combine comedy and transformation and create something called the Wake Up College Tour."

In case you are wondering,
here's what I looked like when I was saying that:

*Also, here's a gentleman reading the front page
of the* New York Times *around the time that I did that
(give or take a year or two) for historical context:*

*All of this was in October 2010, which was about a year and a half
before the 2012 summer Olympics were about to start.
Here's a picture of the opening ceremony.*

What a great time that was! (October 2010, not the summer of 2012.)

That week we made probably four or five hundred videos. That might seem like a lot of work and a lot of time, but because I was excited and pulled toward it, it was actually effortless. During that time I would have been performing in a comedy club, and my mind could see the loss of immediate money and the shallow love that I would have gotten from the audience, so once again my mind felt sad because it was losing something, but my soul was saying, "Trust me on this, we've got something bigger coming through." Within the following couple weeks, many, many, many of the colleges said yes to booking me for a rate of probably three times as much as my comedy club rate. The next thing I knew I was suddenly booked at close to a hundred colleges performing comedy and transformation.

So, in the old days I would make a flat fee to spend Wednesday through Sunday in a comedy club. I couldn't quite say what my soul was feeling, the audience wasn't in alignment with my truth, and there were thousands of other headlining comics in competition with me. Now I can say exactly what my heart wants to say, and I'm doing something that is actually helping the audience. I'm now in a brand-new field and am able to bring in even more income in less time. Bob Proctor says the less replaceable you are, the more you're worth. As I was bringing in all of my unique abilities, I became less replaceable and my value went up. The fulfillment that was shooting through me and the external benefits were so much bigger because I trusted that feeling.

My alignment with myself and my power was changing, and all of a sudden I was in this field with almost no competition, actually doing what my heart wanted me to do. I started doing corporate gigs for all sorts of different companies, speaking at different consciousness and business seminars, speaking at spiritual centers, and all of a sudden I was in higher demand than I had ever been in my life.

It was the craziest feeling to walk away from something that was such a sure thing, and what I had been working toward for so long, and just jump into this unknown . . . and then to find myself totally supported and being brought to a higher level than I had even envisioned. The only reason I say all of this is to let people know that they have the exact same ability to drop the things that are heavy in their life and open up to an entirely new world of possibility. Some people say, "But you're different from me, you had this huge career," but that doesn't matter. These careers are by-products of my leaps. I've seen this happen to people all over the place. The support that you are given when you drop the things in your life that are keeping you stuck and begin allowing a new creative energy to flow through you is actually a real thing. I'm not talking about magic here, it's just nature.

This is what makes life the most exciting thing on the planet for me. It's as if life wants to expand through me. I'm like a tree reaching for the sun, so I guess you are too. There is something that is pulling us forward and calling us into a bigger version of ourselves, and when we go with that flow, we move into alignment with nature itself. When you take a step in a new, exciting direction, that feeling of excitement is your signal that you'll be supported along the way. We often think that taking that leap will be too hard, but what I've found is, it's actually way easier to leap than to stay stagnant when you consider the fact that you'll have tons more energy because you'll be excited, and that life will start to collaborate with you in ways that you can't see before you leap.

As I was doing these colleges that I booked myself, there was a huge, well-known, and powerful booking agency that I was with that wasn't involved in the process of booking the colleges, but they were still taking a commission on the gigs because of the contract I'd signed. So every time a gig would come in, I would immediately feel this requirement that I had to give this agency a percentage of something that they hadn't helped create. Immediately they started feeling heavy. This wasn't a greediness thing; it just felt like an energetic dead end. I started feeling that they were taking from me in a nonreciprocal way that wasn't giving back equal value. My heart told me, even though I didn't understand why, "It's time for me to leave this agency." My mind was horrified and tried to remind me that the agency did do a lot of different things for me: they got me auditions for movies, commercials, and TV shows. If you have to justify why you're doing something, it's not your highest calling. There are all sorts of things that we don't have to rationalize, because they are effortless and are in total alignment with what we're here to do. I don't have to go, "Well, speaking onstage pays well, and people seem to like it, so I guess I'll keep doing it." This is my soul's calling and I don't have to explain it to anybody.

You can hear people justifying when they go, "Yeah, that person was pretty crappy to me, but it was fun when we went to the movies that one time." That's not your soul's calling; that's you apologetically justifying and trying to find some reason to stay in something, and you're only explaining it to yourself because you know that your heart doesn't want it. Whenever we're justifying, we're just trying to hold on to something like a life raft so we don't have to find out what we might be without it, and I found myself doing that with this agency. My heart said, "Let go of this agency; they're not your highest calling. They're taking from you but they're not giving." My mind said, "But they give me auditions for movies, they're really good for me." That's how I knew it was time for me to let go of them.

It was really funny because my mind's biggest reason for not leaving this agency was that they would get me auditions for movies, yet for three years, even though I'd auditioned for movies while I was with that agency, I couldn't book anything. While I was holding on to the agency even though my heart didn't want to, I was in conflict with myself, trying to keep the agency happy and not moving from my soul. So I was blowing it in every audition because I was scared that I would lose the agency. I was people-pleasing and not giving the real me in any audition. Because I had the belief that I needed an agency to get a movie, that belief blocked me from accessing the power that would have brought all of my skills and abilities and childlike creativity into the room.

So I made the call to this agency and I told them I was going to let go of them. They were shocked because they were a huge agency that nobody walked away from. Something in my body said, "I know on paper it doesn't make sense, but you have to let go of them." As soon as I dropped them I felt a total change in my body. I felt a power in my voice; I felt a reminder to myself that I don't need anything to be what I want to be. I was under the illusion that I needed to keep them because I kept thinking that I wasn't enough on my own.

A week later I was asked to speak at an event called GATE with Jim Carrey and Eckhart Tolle. If you don't know who Eckhart Tolle is, he wrote *The Power of Now*. That book has fewer pictures than this one, but I guess it's still pretty good. If you don't know who Jim Carrey is, he's the star of the movie *Ace Ventura*. That movie has less pages than this book, but I guess it's still pretty good. During that performance I was so in my power and alignment that I didn't feel any less worthy to be there than anyone else. I went onstage and said, "This is weird for me because I'm told all the time that I'm what would happen if Jim Carrey and Eckhart Tolle had a baby." I watched as the two of them looked at each other and I said, "I don't know if you guys are picturing this . . . Eckhart, I know you're not because it's a thought, and I know you don't have those." That got a huge laugh, and then I said, "Some of you guys might think that joke was offensive, but it's in the past, so Eckhart doesn't even know about it." That's when the place went crazy; it was like *Showtime at the Apollo*. After that, I had so many producers come up to me and directly offer me movie roles and ask me to be a part of their projects. It was so crazy because it was a week after I had dropped the agency that I was only keeping because they were going to get me movies. While I had them for three years I couldn't get any movies, and as soon as I dropped them and stepped into the power that I had been stifling, I booked everything.

Since I stopped forcing myself to audition for roles, I've actually booked more roles. Since I stopped trying to get love through other people, I've experienced love. Since I stopped trying to get clients to work with me, clients have started coming right to me. Everything you desire will fall into your lap if you just let it. What I've realized is that instead of trying to go get something, our job is to just let ourselves receive the limitless abundance that is available to us by acting on the knowledge that we are totally taken care of and supported no matter what.

At the beginning of this ninety-day challenge I had so many friends give me crap and tease me about it. They said it was extreme and that it was so crazy. By day ninety I had a massively healthy body, a very focused mind-set, a totally new income, and an absolute transformation in my life. I had released many of my addictions. I had an entirely new career and connection to myself. Actually, many of the people who were teasing me ended up deciding to do the same thing. Nobody understands your calling but you. When you feel a calling inside yourself, you just have to do it; you can't check in with other people because they aren't feeling what you're feeling. Listening to that one calling put so many things in store for me, even though the only thing I could see at the beginning was improved health. What I gained was absolute freedom, a totally new understanding of life, the healthiest body I've ever had, movie roles, and basically a new life. All of that was on the other side of just taking the leap and letting go of eating cheese sticks.

Very often we keep things that we think will get us what we want, but they're actually *keeping us* from getting what we truly want. If you want to feel love and you think you need someone or something else so that you can feel love, that is actually going to prevent you from feeling the love that you truly are, and living in that place is the only way to attract someone else who loves themselves too. Your job is to feel the love in you, beyond whatever circumstance your mind is saying you need to have for you to be happy. This life is a playground, it's not a multiple-choice exam. You can't screw this up. Listen to your body, take the leaps that are scary and exciting and calling you from the depths of your soul, and watch how the world unfolds in front of you.

chapter 10

The Very Informative Chapter

chapter 11

Welcome to Deep Down

It's hard to go back into talking about spirituality and consciousness when I know the very last thing you saw in this book was a
giant picture of a baby in a taco. Maybe we should transition back
with pictures of things that are less ridiculous. Here we go . . .

Just a taco.

Okay. Are you ready?

In the chapter before the one with the baby taco, I told the story of the leaps that I had to take and the things that I let go of that brought me to where I am now. I talked about how I had to trust this feeling that I had inside of me, even though I didn't have any external evidence that things would work out the way they did. The real reason I was able to make those leaps was because there was this knowing in me that somehow everything would be okay, no matter what happened.

All the time, we hear people say things like, "Life is really crazy right now, but *deep down* I know everything's going to work out," or "*Deep down* I know I'll be fine, but right now I'm really scared," or "*Deep down* I know there's a reason for this." We say those things as passing phrases in the middle of stressing about something like a breakup or losing a job, and then we dismiss them and go right back to worrying about whatever's going wrong in our lives. But what if *deep down* is actually a place you can live? What if that part of us knows that no matter what we're going through, everything is going to be totally okay in the end? What if *deep down* were your default setting?

When you're saying, "*Deep down* I know everything is going to be okay," you're admitting that there is some kind of knowing inside you that is bigger than whatever part of you is concerned with what is happening in that moment. You're aware that a space of calm is there, but it's so far removed from our experience that we actually call it something different. We say, "Deep down I know that everything is going to be all right," instead of just saying, "I know everything is going to be all right." Or just simply, "Everything's fine." We choose to identify more with the worrying than with the knowing deep inside us.

If we know that place is inside us somewhere, why don't we access it and live from that place all the time? It's probably because our minds don't actually want everything to be okay. Our minds are constantly looking for new problems to solve because problem solving is what our minds are built for. The mind believes that if all of a sudden we didn't have any problems to solve, then it would be out of a job. Then the mind would have to go back to waiting tables and living at its mom's house, which isn't all that bad except that it would have to share a room with its little sister, who is just turning fifteen and is in that phase where she has to act like she hates everything. So obviously, the mind is very motivated to keep fixing problems and acting like you need it more than you actually do. In fact, it's because of this that our minds create problems that aren't even there. They create problems so they have a job to do.

Our minds come up with thousands of reasons why we're not okay in any given moment. We're too fat, we're too skinny, we don't have enough money, we don't have the right relationship, we're not good-looking, we're too good-looking, we don't have enough friends on Facebook, we don't know what Facebook is . . . we're always looking for reasons in our external circumstances to prove why we shouldn't be happy. But with all of these crazy thoughts running around our heads, somewhere underneath all that madness is the knowing that regardless of all of that, we are perfect, we are loved, we are love.

When I was going through all of those leaps and letting go of my old career to make room for something bigger to come through, I never actually knew how it was all going to turn out, and I had tons of thoughts going through my head telling me why I was crazy to give it all up, but the reason I was able to keep moving forward and taking those risks was that I was starting to connect to that deep-down place within myself. I started to more and more use deep down as my jumping-off place instead of my last resort.

Most of us, as a society, choose to not live in that deep-down knowing; instead we live in the shallow place of believing what the mind tells us about ourselves and our circumstances. Because the majority of people are living in that place, when we want to feel connection, instead of just connecting with ourselves deep down, we end up connecting with other people at that shallow level and everyone just ignores that deeper place within themselves. Almost everyone is really just connecting to other people on the level of these external circumstances and not actually experiencing other people fully. That's why many guys connect to each other by watching football instead of sitting in a circle talking about what they are actually feeling. Some guys sit around in circles talking about their feelings, but mostly they are feelings about football.

It's great to connect on those types of things, and there's nothing wrong with football—in fact I recently enjoyed watching a game where some tremendous baskets were made by the goalie. Once he hit the football out of the park he got in his car made by Tide detergent and drove it in circles, then he got out and served a tennis ball to Serena Williams. What a sport football is. However, connecting primarily through things like that has also helped train us to live in this surface level of life and not see beyond the external circumstances into the truth that everything is always working out and that there is never a reason to worry about anything. We buy into the fact that we need to fix the world around us and that there are all of these problems, but underneath that belief is the understanding that everything we see with our eyes is part of the perfection of life that is constantly growing and evolving.

Through things like meditation and my personal experiences, I've become more and more aware of that voice that is always trying to fix things on the surface level of life. I'll probably talk more about meditation later, but as I just sit and watch that voice trying to solve and create problems in my mind, I start to feel the presence of that deep knowing almost wrap around that voice and let it know that everything is going to be okay. It's almost like that voice is a kid that is having a tantrum and *deep down* is like the parent that is just watching and comforting the child. It can do and say the craziest things and deep down just looks at it lovingly. After a while it's almost like your perspective flips, and instead of being the kid looking at the parent, you become the parent looking at the kid. The kid can do anything and it won't change the love that the parent has for them.

What if you knew you could think anything and still be loved? What if you could think the most judgmental, spiteful thing and still be loved? What if you could feel any emotion—anger, rage, guilt—and you'd still be loved no matter what? Well, you can. Your mind will try to convince you that if you think or feel a certain way, you are wrong or bad somehow, but that space deep down is just like a loving parent that will guide you back to the truth that nothing about you is wrong.

It's only our resistance to our thoughts and the mind-made belief that one thought is better than another that keeps us in a cycle of shame, regret, and self-judgment. We often hold on to and hide the things that we are ashamed of; that mental habit is the thing that keeps a belief about ourselves alive and the reason we might repeat those actions that we were ashamed of in the first place. It's like when you a have an exciting secret about a friend's party or something, and even though you can't tell them and try to play it cool, every time you see them it's all you can think about. The more we hold something down, the more it wants to come to the surface.

If you move into that space of deep down and start to move from the perspective that loves everything about you, you can allow all of those things you're ashamed of to come to the surface and allow them to be loved and accepted. As a by-product they will actually lose the power you've given them and will start to dissolve. It's like a bully who feeds on someone getting annoyed and putting up a fight—as soon as you don't react to the bully and even find things that you like about them, your relationship loses its dynamic and it's not fun for them to pick on you anymore. I wish I knew that in middle school.

So these thoughts can show up one after another, and if you're more connected to deep down than the belief that you are those thoughts, you'll start to find that those thoughts don't own you the way they used to. You won't be afraid of them anymore, and instead of picking up some addictive thing to distract you from those thoughts, you'll be able to connect to the space that can totally see through all of those illusions.

So, what's changed for me over the last several years is that instead of just visiting deep down in those moments of chaos, I'm starting to actually live in deep down. It's actually possible to live in a place of not just optimism or positivity, but an actual experiential knowing that nothing can go wrong and nothing you think or feel is wrong. It's a place of total acceptance of yourself and others that gives you a safe space where your mind can become creative and expansive instead of living in fear of repression and shame.

Instead of deep down being like this beautiful summer home that you only peek through the window of when you're stressed and the rest of the time you live in a cramped studio apartment that smells like cat pee, why don't you make the beautiful summer home your *home*? I know the studio apartment is familiar, and over time you've kind of gotten used to the cat pee, but wouldn't it be nice to have a couple extra bedrooms and no cat pee for once?

It's our job to start living in deep down before we do anything else. Instead of living in chaos, when you start to live in deep down, problems will start to disappear because you'll realize that many of the problems you had were really just in your mind. You start to move from a foundation that is rooted in natural optimism and excitement for life instead of having to manipulate your external circumstances in a way that finally allows you to feel freedom and peace for a moment. We can't take truly powerful and meaningful action in this world until we have transcended the mind's need to fix and solve the endless surface-level problems that it creates.

But what if deep down wasn't a place to live, and it was actually just what you were? Stay tuned . . .

chapter 12

Universally Selfish

So we're somewhere around halfway through this book and I think that's something to celebrate. They celebrate getting to halfway at pretty much everything: Broadway shows have intermission with drinks and candy, sporting events have halftime shows with cheerleaders and fireworks, and whenever you're halfway through making out with a woman, she stops you and offers you celebration gum. So, I figured maybe we should do something to really make this a special moment for both of us. I think I have the perfect thing to really turn up the heat on this halfway point. What do you think it is? Here's a hint, it's a crossword puzzle:

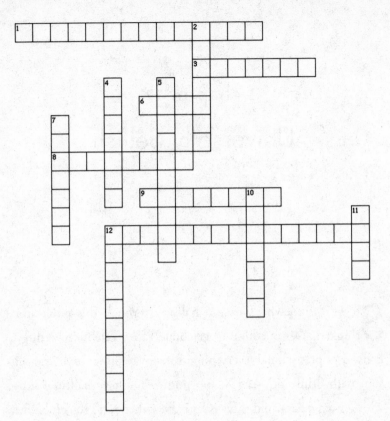

Across

1. What I was at the beginning of this book

3. Something you're missing out on by reading this book

6. What a baby is in most of the time

8. Lao-tzu says to remove this to access full freedom

9. The best taco place with the freshest ingredients around

12. What this thing is

Down

2. Inventor of the lightbulb and sixteenth president of the United States
4. Kyle's delicious snack from chapter five
5. The key ingredient to Taco Time's tacos
7. The worst brand of tortilla chips
10. The capital of Wisconsin
11. How strong Kyle is
12. It's not quite cheese and it's not quite cake

If you were able to finish it, take a picture of yourself with it and email it to crossword@kylecease.com and I'll send you something very special. It might just be another crossword puzzle, or possibly the same one, I don't know yet, but it will definitely be very special, or it possibly won't be, I can tell you that much.

Other than the crossword celebration, the fact that we're at the halfway point is important for another reason . . .

The first half of this book has been helping to get you and me out of our old stories and limited perspective of who we think we are and what we think we're capable of. As we transition into the second half of the book, we're going to move way beyond any story we could create for ourselves into an even freer and deeper place of understanding what we are and enter a place of effortless being, which will allow us to harness our true creative power and help bring our gifts to the world. I really see what I do as a mission to help people move out of their mind-made illusions of limitation so that they can discover who they truly are, allowing them to start moving in harmony with life and the planet. As a by-product, we will actually begin to shift this world together.

When we start from a place of actual connection to ourselves, every action that we take is in alignment with the laws of nature and what we create in our lives is in service to the world. We don't take more than we need and we give our gifts without worrying about what we'll get for it. There's no external reward that is more fulfilling than being in service to the world. I don't mean that in a corny, sappy way; it actually, literally just feels better. There's nothing more selfish than being selfless. What I mean by that is, when you finally realize that you're infinite and that we are all actually, truly connected, changing the world is a *universally* selfish act.

Even in giving completely, you're still benefiting. That's why it feels good to help someone else: you're actually helping yourself. I'm not talking about people-pleasing here, I'm talking about following your highest calling and honoring the true gifts that are constantly trying to come through you for the benefit of everyone.

Being selfish in a universal way means you are making yourself a priority so that you can overflow your power, love, and compassion onto the world. Every self-help book uses this example, but there really is a truth to the fact that you need to put the oxygen mask on yourself first before you can help anyone else. What those books don't mention is Nickelback.

Being selfish in an *egoic* way keeps you confined to the idea that you are separate and small. It means you're *sacrificing* your highest calling and connection to yourself in order to get something or not lose something. This is like trying to hand other people your oxygen mask while asking them to give you *their* oxygen.

As you keep going deeper into yourself, you start making decisions from "What does the world want?" instead of "What do I, the individual, want?" Your body starts rewiring itself to see itself as part of the whole, and the decisions that you make are always moving from the world's highest calling. For example, when you're being *universally selfish* and you see someone who's cute, if it's not the highest calling for the consciousness of the world, you won't even be attracted to that person. But if you see yourself as separate, you might want to date that person in order to "complete you" and add to the separate story that you believe you are, even if it's not in the best interest of your purpose, your calling, their calling, or the world.

Eventually, you start to stop seeing yourself as a separate person, and more and more, you start to see yourself as the whole world. You're always really moving from the same amount of selfishness, it's just that as your awareness grows, you start to serve a higher intention and purpose. We're all seeking our highest happiness, and as I start to see myself as the whole world, I won't get my highest happiness from eating Taco Time. I'll need to do something that is actually in alignment with the way that life wants to express itself through me for the benefit of everything. And that's how you become universally selfish.

So get excited about where this is going and about the fact that, through reading this, you are raising your awareness and moving into expansion and alignment with the universe, which will actually benefit you as an individual in all ways. When you start to align with universal principles, your health goes through the roof, your income rises, your relationships thrive, and everything really just figures itself out without your even trying.

What we are is way beyond any of the boundaries that we've boxed ourselves into, and knowing this allows creative ideas and visions for the future to come in from that out-of-the-box place. We're now moving with the flow of life instead of against it. We're letting ourselves be pulled by inspired ideas and moving into action in the most effortless ways, which allows us to create even more impact in this world than we ever thought possible.

So, in the last chapter I left you with a cliffhanger. I'm sorry it took so long to get back to that point; I'm not good at cliffhangers. We were talking about that place we refer to as deep down and at the end I said, "What if deep down wasn't a place to live, and it was actually just what you were?" More on that in the next chapter.

chapter 13

The Unlucky Chapter

I was just about to actually answer the cliffhanger that I left the last two chapters on, then I realized that this was chapter thirteen and that thirteen is an unlucky number, and lots of buildings don't have a thirteenth floor because of superstitions. So, just to be safe . . .

chapter 14

Are You Ice or Water?

Okay, here we go:

What if deep down wasn't a place to live, and it was actually just what you were?

I'm often asked the question "How do I get into the moment?" This is like a fish asking, "How do I get into water?"

You are the moment. The second you think it's a place to get to, you cut it off in your mind and create a false obstacle to overcome. Your mind is contained within this moment. Your thoughts, your fears, your goals are all contained inside of this moment.

Whether you like it or not, you are completely, always, only in the now. It will never be something you are able to achieve. Even when you are chasing it, you are in the now. Nothing from your past is ever bigger than now.

You might have a lot of moments from your past that feel amazing. Maybe you can sit and remember a concert. Maybe you remember when you fell in love. Maybe you remember an incredible vacation. You might think the reason you felt so good was because of the external things around you, but that's not the case. The reason you felt so good was that, for a little while, you completely let go of your addiction to your mind and experienced the moment that you were in fully. You got out of the way of your connection to yourself. These external things were catalysts for you to give yourself permission to feel all of yourself without your thoughts of past and future getting in the way.

As you allow yourself to stop trying to get anywhere and fully accept everything that is coming up, you will discover that there is nowhere to get to. Your mind might bring up a thought, and your job is to just love the thought, not cater to it.

Example . . .

Let's say you're sitting on your favorite, or even second-favorite, sofa, and a thought comes up. The thought is this: "OH NO. I HAVE A JOB INTERVIEW NEXT WEEK. WHAT IF I THROW UP ON THE INTERVIEWER'S DESK?"

If you choose to see that thought as a little child and you just tell the thought that you hear it and love it, it will go away. Really picture that when that thought comes up as if it's a child who said it to you. If a kid came up to you and said, "What if I throw up on the desk?" you'd just be there for them, hear their concerns, and let them express their emotions. You wouldn't be afraid of them, you wouldn't run away, you wouldn't ignore them with an addiction, and you wouldn't agree with them and start worrying. You'd just love them and let them know it's going to be okay, and once they knew that, their fear would go away. If you ignored them, though, they'd just get louder and louder and start to freak out. When you become a space of love for any thought that arises within you, you can literally feel the thought moving through you. Your true acceptance of a passing thought is actually what allows it to just keep passing through.

What's fascinating about this is that these thoughts that are coming up are literally you as a child. These are thoughts that were never able to be fully expressed around people in your past because of a fear of danger or not being accepted. To make sure you are safe and accepted, you continue repressing these thoughts, and they will keep coming up over and over until you finally decide to accept that part of yourself. It's the repressing of our thoughts that causes our addictive behavior. It's the repressing of our childhood self from the past that makes us feel at war with ourselves, so we look for an addiction to numb the pain.

The truth is, that painful past childhood story doesn't exist anymore. It's an illusion. There is only this moment. In this moment, you might be thinking about the past, and if you are in resistance to the thoughts that are coming up, it will seem like your past might never leave. Every single painful memory or emotion from our past is just arising in this moment so that we can learn to surrender on a new level.

Whenever you're not accepting and are in resistance to a past story, it's like you're watching a movie and arguing with it. You're like a crazy old person standing up in a movie theater yelling at the screen. So you're deciding to fight with this movie that doesn't actually exist, but because you're fighting with it, you're making it real and you are giving it power over you. Even then, you're still in the moment. You're still always in the now, even when you're in the illusion of the past, even when you're caught up in the story. What's so cool about this is that now, even when you're in a battle with the illusions of your mind, you can start to connect to the space that all of that is happening in and choose to respond to the movie however you want.

Your past has happened. That's a fact. It's up to you to decide whether you want to be in an argument with yourself. The only way to move forward is to accept it. Truly, truly, truly accept it, which can only be done in this moment. Or you can just realize it's a movie and enjoy it . . . which is actually a way to accept it.

A great exercise that I do with the people I work with is to say any fear-based thought that's coming up and then say "and I love that" right afterward. If you allow a thought to show up and consciously acknowledge it and give it love, you short-circuit the pattern of resistance that keeps those kinds of thoughts active. I do this all the time. If I'm going onstage or doing something that might bring up a thought like "I'm afraid they won't like me," I just turn it into "I'm afraid they won't like me, and I love that." This allows me to accept that thought and move beyond it, instead of fighting it and getting trapped underneath it.

It's important that "and I love that" isn't just empty words though. There's a feeling in your body that happens when you actually become okay with a fearful thought. It's a feeling of release from the limitation that thought is creating in you. Try this on your own: if there's any thought that has been coming up for you recently that is causing you stress, say it out loud and then say, "and I love that." If you can't think of anything, say, "I can't think of anything, and I love that."

The first couple times you do it, you might feel like it's inauthentic, or like you're just trying to trick yourself, but this isn't some positivity exercise where you try to convince yourself that everything is fine when it's not. This is about accessing the part of yourself that truly loves every part of you. This is about embodying the knowing that everything actually is okay, and it's only the fearful, scared-child part of you that is afraid in the first place. It's about moving beyond the pictures that our minds show us and starting to access the infinite number of solutions to all of the challenges that life brings us.

You might be thinking, "But I don't love that." If that's how you *choose* to feel, then you will create a resistance that will cause that feeling to stay there for as long as it needs to, until you decide to love yourself on a whole new level. Everything that you haven't loved is actually an invitation for yourself to discover a new level of self-acceptance. This level of acceptance might seem scary because you haven't been there before, but the second you truly say yes to it, you will never want to go back. The lack of acceptance means that you have just located pockets of resistance in your body that you are about to replace with self-love and care. Get excited. Think of how powerful you will feel when you choose to accept this thing that you have potentially spent years resisting.

We're used to connecting to what we can see. We can see thoughts floating around in our heads, we can see the people around us in our lives, and we can see our pasts on the movie screens of our minds. But our real power shows up when we start to connect to what we can't see. If you were swimming in the ocean, you might instinctively want to be safe and stay near the shore, but actual possibility starts to open up when you move beyond the shore and start to move further out, away from safety. Your actual power, your actual creativity, your actual love, isn't found in the shallow thoughts that your past story shows you; it's in the uncertainty and unlimited potential of what's beyond all of that. Most people live their entire lives just wading near the shore. We now have the opportunity and the awareness to discover an entirely new world of possibility that starts once we *leave* the shallow waters.

Every single day, when I wake up, I sit comfortably with my eyes closed for two hours. I love to sit and listen and love the many, many thoughts that come up within my awareness. I sit, watch, and accept. The longer I sit there, the more I realize that I am not these thoughts, but I am much more the *space* that these thoughts are inside of.

What is this space? It's infinite possibility. It's freedom. It's love. It's everything. It's never-ending creativity. It's me.

I am all of this, and so are you.

As I move beyond the limitations of my thoughts, my emotions, my past, my story, my fears, and my body, I realize that I am something eternal and my job is to allow myself to connect to this place that is always here, whether I know it or not.

This place is the deep-down space that we know we can connect to. We are actually always connected to it, we just can't see it when we obsess over our thoughts by judging them. Once we let go of our addiction to the illusion of our limitations, we can slowly dissolve into the space that we actually are.

When we are stressed out and lost in that illusion, sometimes it can feel like the world is crushing us. We feel the strain in our heads as we do everything we can to keep things from falling apart. It's almost like we are these fragile ice cubes that are melting into a glass of warm water. We feel separate and small and like we have to keep it all together or we'll lose everything. We feel like we are getting smaller and smaller and if we don't do something quick, if we don't fight, if we don't run, we will cease (MY NAME!) to exist.

What if the truth is that we are more like the warm water than the ice cube? What if you could be a space for your fear to dissolve into? What if you were a giant glass of warm water that could love and connect with the fear inside of you? The ice will eventually melt into the water, but if you thought your identity was ice, you would try as hard as you could to stay frozen because you'd think melting meant death. You would have to be more rigid, cold, and hard as a protective mechanism if you believed that you were ice.

What ice might not understand is, if it would surrender to the warm water, it would melt, but it would still exist. Not only would it still exist, but it would join together with even more of itself and access an entirely new level of possibility. If the ice cube would just sit back and let itself go, it would slowly dissolve back into what it actually is, a warm, fluid, soft glass of water.

When we are in fear, we are often scared of the love that we are. We are scared to receive love from others and we are unaware that it is inevitable that we will become love.

When you are scared of something, you are like the ice cube. You believe that you have something to protect and you are trying to sustain an old identity. At any moment, you can let go and fall into the love that you are. You can be the water that holds the space for the ice. You are the love that holds the space for the thoughts.

You have nothing to do. It's being done for you.

chapter 15

Let Yourself Melt

After I wrote chapter fourteen, I went to the gym and grabbed an amazing lunch at an incredible vegan restaurant called Joi Cafe in Thousand Oaks, California. You might think that has nothing to do with this book, and in some ways you're right.

The reason I'm talking about it is because I *love* putting my money into any company that is moving from universal principles. Companies like this are *universally selfish* and are here not only for profit, but for the service of the world. I talk about this more in my next book, *The Entrepreneurial Shift*. (I hope you read this far, Michele. And guess what, it's already written. I mean, I probably still need to go through it and make some changes to update it, but it's pretty much done.) This restaurant is supporting local farming, and every purchase I make at restaurants like this and other healthy organic places sends a message to everyone that we only support something that moves the truth forward. I feel good when I do it, and the clarity I feel from doing something so in alignment with the universe allows me to access even faster ideas.

During both lunch and my workout, my mind could not stop coming up with more about the comparison of water and ice to love and fear. It's my new favorite metaphor. My heart was screaming so many new ideas and points at me the entire time.

It's so funny because as I started the water-and-ice analogy I had no idea what kind of door I was opening. It just felt good to write about water and ice and let the truth unfold as I went. It was like I was dipping my toes in what I thought was a couple of inches of water and discovered an entire ocean. I seriously can't stop with the water-themed metaphors now. I wonder if it's just because I'm sweaty from working out.

For two hours now, I've picked up tons of new insights, and now I can't stop writing. I had to take the food to go because I am feeling kind of possessed and have to share more. Something is doing the work through me; I truly feel like I am just a messenger. I can tell you that the more I tap into the water, the more I see that the possibilities of this go on forever. As my ice melts, I move from being a separate cube floating in a sea, looking for other cubes to stay connected to so that I can stay cold, into water, as I discover an entire ocean of ideas and creativity that seems to be never ever ending.

As I wrote about the ice and the water, my ice was actually melting with each word that poured out. Just from experiencing and learning from what I was writing as I was writing it, I've been dissolving even more into infinite possibility. Today I am writing you with more fluidity, and I am connected to even more of myself than I ever have been before.

I am still in my gym clothes and I haven't even opened my bag of food yet. It's kind of funny because at the beginning of this book, food was my number one addiction to distract me from my creativity, and now I can't even take a break to eat because I'm so pulled by this. I am getting so much joy from the discovery of what is coming through me. I can't stop writing and discovering myself right now. I'm just passionately excited to share this with you because I want you to know that if something that your soul is calling you to do seems hard at first, just stay with it, because it has the potential to lead you to the most effortless freedom you've ever experienced.

Let yourself just drop the illusion that you've been trying to protect your entire life and open up to the idea that everything will be totally fine without it. The ice cube cannot do anything compared to what the entire ocean is capable of. You are the entire ocean.

So right now, your ego (ice) might be asking, "Okay, so how do I become water?" There is no way for the ice to do the work of becoming the water. Think about it: The part of you that wants to change is the ice. Any work that the ice is doing is actually keeping the ice alive. The ice can't sustain itself while at the same time allowing itself to melt.

There is nothing that the ice can do. However, if you do more waterish things, you will melt. Let's talk about this.

Obviously, the ice has to constantly work its ass off to stay ice. Fear has to worry continually to sustain itself. Anything that might speed up the melting process is horrifying and means death to the fear. Fear is scared to look itself in the eye. Fear likes to blame everyone else for hurting it. Fear wants war. Fear wants guns and violence. Fear wants to be right instead of happy. Fear needs to be around other fear to sustain itself.

Ice has to constantly create a freezing situation to live. Fear is the same way.

Guess why the media is always showing you the selected horrifying stories of the world. The media is like a giant freezer. It's no coincidence that many people who are angry watch the news all day in their home. They need that fear for their stories to survive; they need fear so their ice doesn't melt.

People who are in fear have to surround themselves with others who are in fear. People who complain about everything must be around other fear-based people to keep their ice cube frozen. When fear-based people are around people who are self-connected, they feel threatened. Water can remind ice that everything is okay, and that would mean that the ice is *wrong*. The worst thing to someone in fear is to be wrong. People who are in fear think that being wrong means death. They would rather fight, and even kill, others than face the fact that there is more to life than what they believe.

If the media is like a freezer, then nature is like a stove. If you go out into nature for a couple of weeks, your ice cube will dissolve into your infinite potential pretty damn fast. People are often scared to do something without their phones. That's because your phone, Facebook, and other distractions can often keep you connected to other freezerlike situations and give you permission to stay identified as ice.

If you were to go for at least ten days phoneless, medialess, and without other people who act like ice cubes, you would melt very, very quickly. You would be like a boiling pot of water and you would feel your old identity dissolve into the infinite space of possibility and creativity that you are. You would feel expansion and love. You would feel a new level of fulfillment while also feeling a sense of letting go. There would be sadness as you mourned the old story of who you thought you were. You would feel tears as you said good-bye to the old protective mechanisms that helped you through a challenging world and a difficult childhood. You would say good-bye to the old story of protection that did what it had to do to not feel abandoned or yelled at, or ignored or hurt by your parents. You would feel that ice cube that you might have identified with for years dissolve into the real you. It would dissolve into your infinite ocean.

You would not have to protect yourself anymore. You are the guidance and the protection that loves that little child, and it would finally know that it was safe and surrender to itself. Nature, meditation, creativity, love, and connecting with other warm-water-like people is the fastest way to melt your ice cube and connect with the sea of the infinite.

Wow, I'm still not done with this metaphor . . .

The world's collective water is figuratively warmer than it used to be, meaning the awareness of the world is rising. It's really amazing. As the climate is literally getting warmer, our collective awareness is also growing. As we are becoming more aware, more compassionate, more patient, and more forgiving, we are becoming warmer and are connecting to each other in a way we never have before.

If you are reading this book, especially this far, you are probably a pretty warm glass of water right now. You are open to discovering that your old way of thinking might not be the only way. You are open to new possibilities and you are learning beyond your story. It would be impossible for you to read this while staying frozen. You can already relax into the idea that you are pretty freaking thawed out.

There are people who are still rigid and cold in this ocean of possibility, but they are melting faster. Some people are holding on for dear life. They are almost certain that they are these ice cubes and they have to find some way to survive as the water around them is getting warmer. The more they hold on to their ice, the more desperate and extreme they become.

Overall, we are now too warm to support hate. It will be impossible for ice-cube-based governments to control us with fear. They are only able to control ice cubes because many people on this planet have become water and they are not scared. Fear is becoming a dying phenomenon and it's melting exponentially faster and faster. Even some of the people who are controlling have become water and don't want to control anymore.

You know that a half-melted ice cube in a warm glass of water will melt much faster as it gets smaller. We are melting into the infinite so quickly, and it's possible that even though it took us years to start melting, it might only take us months, weeks, or even days to completely finish dissolving.

The world is too warm to support world wars, violence, and worldwide hate. Just from reading this chapter, you are raising your own awareness. This raises the temperature another 0.1 degrees, because what you learn cannot be unlearned. You know that you are infinite, so it would be impossible for you to move like an ice cube for more than a few minutes now. You are another space of love and support and you are infinite possibility.

We have moved to a time where the only way for you to thrive in any area of your life is to move like water. You have to tap into your greatness. Your business, relationships, creativity, and health all require your self-connection to the ocean. There is no other way around it. Ice might have worked in the past, but it won't anymore. Love yourself. It's time to move forward. It's only scary because we have not been here before. It's much scarier to stay the same way.

One way to immediately apply this new awareness in your everyday life is to stop identifying yourself as the ice, as the scared little child who turned into an ice cube out of fear. When we say "I," we're almost always referring to an illusion; we're talking about the fearful ice-cube story that our minds have created about us. There's a really simple way that we can start to switch that around and begin to identify with the totality of who we are much more than we identify with our limited fearful beliefs. Here's an exercise that will help you to move even more from a fearful ice-cube-like state into water:

We've been talking about the idea that deep down isn't somewhere to get to, it's what you are. There's never a place to get to. If you're feeling pain it's only because there is a belief standing between you and your total freedom. If we're used to saying, "I'm really stressed, but I know deep down everything's all right," the only reason we're in pain in that situation is that we're identified with the "stress" instead of the "all right." If you think who you are is the stress, then you're going to do everything you can to keep it alive. We can start to rewire our awareness just by flipping that around and saying, "I know everything is all right, but my brain is stressed." Even something as simple as switching the way you refer to yourself and what you identify as "you" is enough to start to move your awareness from ice to water. Eventually you will actually be able to feel, in your body, that the stress happening in your mind is just part of a protective story and there's an entirely different dimension within you that isn't stressing at all.

Try this for yourself: Think about something you might be worrying or stressing about, and feel how that stress is really only happening in your brain. If you listen to your heart—and I mean that like feel your body, feel your chest, feel your core you'll notice that your stress isn't happening there, it's just in your head. Now ask your heart what it thinks about that issue that you're worried about. Take a second and close your eyes and feel what your heart has to say to you.

Any time I actually stop and listen to my heart, I always get an answer like "It's going to be fine" or "This doesn't matter," or more often, it's just "I love you." That's all we ever want, right? To be loved? Isn't it crazy that all we have to do is step out of the chaos of our minds for a second and pay attention to our hearts and we get what we've been craving our entire lives? That level of certainty and security is always there, right underneath everything we've been taught we need to be worried about. The water that your ice cube is floating in is actually the safety that it's been trying to find the entire time.

So actually, actually do this. Allow yourself to hear what your heart is really feeling, and when you notice what your heart is saying, change that to "I." This isn't just a cute exercise; that voice is actually you. It's your truth in this moment. The evidence of that is that the stress you are usually identified with is always only based off the past. Your mind is always bringing either the past or the future into this moment to distract you from the truth that everything is actually okay.

You're never ever scared right now, you're always just pulling in past fears or worthiness issues, like "They might not like me (because I've never been worthy)" or "What if I mess this up (like last time)," and believing those thoughts are the truth. This means those thoughts are not you; that's the past you. In this moment, nothing is actually wrong. You are just this moment. You are the infinite possibility that this moment holds. If you change your perception to "My past story is worried they might not like me, but I know I'm just pure love," you'll shift into a space that is connected to endless possibility, regardless of the lies that show up in your mind. And also, everything that the mind is trying to make wrong in this moment is actually just a part of the perfection that you are.

Don't go to the next chapter without sitting and doing this for a little while. Take out a piece of paper and write down a few of your fears or something you might be worried about that's coming up in the next few days. As you write, notice where you feel the fears coming from and allow your heart to respond. Realize that voice that is responding is actually *you* responding to the fear. Notice that it's just a habit to say, "I'm scared . . . ," and rearrange the sentence from the point of view of what you actually are. Within minutes the fear will lose its power over you because it was your identification with the fear that kept it alive. Your belief was that without the fear, you'd be nothing. The truth is, you're the love that the fear needed to finally relax and melt into the water that it actually is.

Let's thrive together and explore this ocean. Metaphor complete.

chapter 16

Don't Ask HOW Ever Again

Remember when you started this book and thought you were a separate person? LOL. Now you're a freaking ocean. Just take that in for a second. Fifteen chapters ago we were worried about some small thing like if you were going to get to date that person or how you were going to get out of debt. I was worried about writing a book and saw no possible way that I could accomplish that. Now what has happened has been so much bigger than anything that I could have come up with. I am so thankful that I didn't have a vision for what the book was going to be, because the greatest vision I could have ever come up with would have been me back when I was a little ice cube. In fact, here is my baby picture.

While I was writing chapter two, a friend came by and took a picture of me. Here's that picture:

Here's a selfie I took today:

Now I am aware that I am so much bigger and connected to everything. I don't know anything about what will happen with this book, or my entire life, and I truly, truly love that.

As we discover that there is this giant ocean of untapped possibility that we can connect to in every moment, our external goals are now becoming secondary and our number one goal is to move into that connected state of oceanlike being. I know I said the water metaphor was complete; it looks like I was wrong.

By stepping outside of the ego and expanding our awareness, we're moving much more into a state of being than a state of doing. This is a place where we're not taking actions that are motivated by fear, a need to fix, or protection. Instead, we are slowing down and starting to tune into what our heart is truly feeling and saying. Many of our questions about what to do or how to get somewhere should be starting to fall away as they are replaced with a call to move inward and just connect with that space of love inside ourselves.

If you're currently not happy with the circumstances of your life, the only reason for that is you've been trying to figure out how to make things happen from an ice cube's perspective. Realize that within that limited, boxed-in perspective, you can only make decisions and create goals based on what the ice cube can see. The more you connect to this moment, the more you'll start to raise your antenna and begin picking up signals that are way beyond the limited story you've been trapped in.

Our mission is starting to change from "How can I create the best career?" or "How can I get the best relationship?" to "How can

I connect to myself more and start to move in alignment with what life is truly calling through me?" Our job now is to really start creating the practice of being and realizing that all of the thoughts that are trying to get us to do things, fix things, and figure things out are really just distractions that are keeping us trapped in the prison of our minds. The only things we should be doing now are things that move us toward being.

If we are in a place of being, then we're more fully connected to what we are in this moment. When we understand that we're just this moment, we're able to receive ideas and opportunities that we otherwise might ignore if we believed that we are our pasts. If you understand that you are the infinite possibility that this moment holds, then no challenge is too big for you to handle. In fact, in that space, you really don't have challenges anymore because any challenge is something that's outside of you and it's only triggering the limited ice part of you. Water isn't triggered by challenges; it flows over or around any obstacle in its path.

Everything that arises in this moment becomes an opportunity for you to grow and expand into even more of yourself. At a certain point, you really start to understand that the true value we receive in any situation is actually the internal growth that brings us closer to knowing that we are just love. That's what we're really after. We're not after the cars, the houses, the relationships, or the fame. Deep down, we truly just want to know *what we are*. When we're chasing those things, we're not actually trying to get those things, we're trying to get the feeling we believe those things will give us. Really though, the idea that we need those things is just the excuse we use to delay us from accessing that feeling right now. All we really want is to know that we are love and to actually experience that. We can know that we are just love intellectually, but our soul is pulling us to actually embody and align with the truth of what we are by moving that way and creating that invincibility. And trust me, the cars, the relationships, the houseboats, and the hot sauce collections will all take care of themselves on levels far beyond what you could ever imagine.

Making it our number one priority to access that place of love first releases us from the prison of our ice cubes. Once we've moved into that place of oneness, we can start to move into action again, but now our action will stem from the awareness of the unlimited possibility that the entire ocean has. We want to move from being into action, from love into doing, not the other way around. Almost the entire world is *doing* so that one day they can *get love*. We know that we *are* love, and now everything we do is infused with that power, that guidance, that knowing. Once we've accessed that love inside of ourselves, everything we do will be bringing love into the world and helping lead others back to that truth within themselves.

Moving into that place of love within ourselves is actually really easy. If you believe that it's hard, that's the problem. That's how ice sees things; it has a belief it won't let go of that keeps it rigid and closed off to possibility. Unfortunately for the ice, it's the easiest thing to become water. It's what you are. Even if you've been totally trapped in the prison of your past story for fifty years, it doesn't take fifty years to get out of it. Awareness doesn't take time, it just takes awareness. You can choose right now to enter a place of being by deciding to listen to your heart instead of listening to the story in your head that is trying to tell you there is something to fix.

In every moment, you make the choice to either move into the illusion of yourself or move into the love that you actually are. Every step you take is either moving you toward the ice cube or moving you toward the ocean. You'll know which is which because it always takes effort to move into the illusion; there's always something you have to do. It takes effort to turn on the TV, to smoke a cigarette, to eat a bag of chips. It never takes any effort to feel your heart and access the love that it's continually pouring out. It's actually always harder, short term *and* long term, to follow the addictions of your ego; we've just gotten really good at blindly following the direction of the mind without questioning its leadership capabilities. The ego has this way of convincing us that we really want to do that addictive thing, but we never actually feel fulfilled or expansive after doing it. It's almost as if your egoic self is this fire that is always asking you to pour gasoline on it, even though it burns you every time. Every time you listen to it, the fire gets bigger and hurts worse. But for some reason it is always asking for more.

If you just stop pouring gasoline on it, the fire will eventually go out and you'll be able to actually feel your heart and receive guidance that is *easier* both in the short term and the long term. The actions that you start to take will be exciting and fun and create the type of exponential results that can only come from a level of creativity that is in alignment with the true creative nature of your entire being.

I've experienced this 100 percent. Following my internal calling and doing something that is actually what my heart wants to do is way easier and is creating results that are way beyond what I ever achieved when I was doing things that were more based in ego. Not just in terms of money, but in terms of fulfillment, impact, and overall happiness. When I'm following my calling, everything just feels effortless and the next step is always obvious.

When your mind is asking HOW to do something, it's just trying to figure out how to fix a feeling of lack that *it* created in the first place. It thinks that it needs to do something right to get the love that it believes it's separate from. When you become aware of that and enter a place of being, you move from a HOW to a WHY.

When you're in a WHY, you're guided by the universe and there is something that is trying to come through you that *has* to be expressed. A powerful WHY will blindside you when you're in a state of being. You'll just be sitting in nature or quietly in your room and it will hit you like a ton of bricks and become your obsession. You can't find your WHY; that's actually something that your ego is trying to do and achieve. A WHY chooses you when you're in alignment and finally able to receive the mission and growth that it has for you.

When your WHY is big enough, it will figure out all the HOWs for you. When you are driven by a WHY, you almost have no work to do anymore. The question "HOW, or WHAT, do I do?" won't even appear anymore. Everything needed to support your WHY will just show up and present you with things that you will feel called and inspired to do. You'll be fueled by an excitement and you won't need to ask anyone's advice. When you're in a WHY, something is coming through that expands the story of you and makes it effortless to step into your highest potential.

So you can always know that you're coming from a limited perspective if you're asking, "HOW do I do this?" You're only asking that because that thing isn't actually your highest calling. Asking that question is actually looking for a reason *not* to do it (for example, "Well, I don't know how to write a book, so I won't"). When you have an exciting idea that comes from your heart, it will pull you off the couch so quickly that you won't even be able to keep up with all of the thousands of HOWs it will throw at you. Those HOWs won't feel like a job, they'll be the only thing you want to do. In that place of excitement, focusing on any addiction or distraction will actually be harder than focusing on the ideas that show up out of inspiration.

If you've ever tried writing a song or a blog, or doing anything creative, and you asked, "Okay, how should I do this?" or "What should I write about?" you probably noticed how hard it was to come up with something that felt exciting. You've probably also experienced a time where an idea actually did pull you off the couch and you couldn't stop yourself from writing or creating that thing. The excitement totally took over and the process of creating was effortless because you were moving with the flow of what wanted to be expressed through you in that moment. What if you could live like that? What if you could just be constantly pulled into giving your gift and guided into that next step in your evolution? What if everything you did was so exciting because it expanded you past your limited story, and by acting on it, you grew and discovered even more of yourself?

If you've ever been at a table with your friends and you said something that was headliner-level funny, it's because you were in that place of effortless creativity and just having fun. In that moment you were water and you opened yourself up to something that took you and the people around you totally into your bodies and into a state of being. Almost all of our amazing creative moments come through when we're in that state of fluid water and we're just playing.

So your job now is to start the practice of fully surrendering and trusting that there is a calling that is always trying to get through to you, and become aware that it can't get our attention when we're a blocked ice cube living in a place of survival. Your job is to move into the ocean and act on everything that inspires you so that you can live in your WHY and give your gift to the world. It's your job to start listening to the calling that expands you instead of the egoic, addictive impulses that shrink you.

I've talked in this book about taking leaps and the different things in my career that I had to let go of to open up the possibility of something new. A leap can be scary, but on the other side of it is growth and new opportunities that you can't see until you take that leap. Even though it's actually the easiest thing we can do, moving into being is really the ultimate leap. It's a leap that you take over and over again in each consecutive moment. It can feel scary to step out of the story of your mind because it's all you've known your entire life, but on the other side of it is an entirely *new* life that will access your infinite potential and pull you into new levels of greatness. So in each moment you can ask yourself, "Will I risk letting go of my old limiting story to leap into my infinite potential?" It's a lot less scary when you put it that way.

All of this endless creativity, excitement, and inspiration becomes available to you as the result of just being and connecting to yourself. It's so simple. It's really the only thing that matters; everything after that is just playing and effortless creation. When you stop allowing yourself to be pulled into the addictions, habits, and distractions that keep you believing that we need to constantly be getting and fixing, you drop all of your resistance and allow that creativity to come through. If there's any ice in you that is still worried . . . just so you know, the fulfilling career, the great relationships, and the incredible health are all just by-products of the being.

So, even though this book is going to move into all sorts of ways to harness the endless creativity that comes out of this place of being, being is still the most important thing. This place of being is the launchpad for everything that comes after it. It's your resting place, it's your home base. If you're ever worried about what you should do, just go into being. Just sit and step back into the awareness that everything you are worried about is simply an illusion that is only painful to the part of yourself that believes it is separate from the love at your core. That illusion that you buy into is the only thing that can be hurt. What you are at your core can never be hurt. The only things that can ever be hurt are your past story, your false presentation of yourself, and your expectations.

When you go through a breakup, you often say, "That person broke my heart." They didn't actually break your heart though, they broke your expectations. By breaking your expectations, they actually moved you *closer* to your heart.

One thing that can help you understand and embody that what you are can't actually be hurt is to just spend time sitting and connecting to that part of yourself. Just sitting and being is such a simple thing, but it also means that a part of your story is going to die, so there *can* be sadness that happens. Just sitting on the couch and absolutely doing nothing but connecting to yourself can make your ego go crazy and try to make you think that this is a big mistake. To your mind, sitting and doing nothing is taking away its control over you, but this is actually the equivalent of your cocoon. It's death to the caterpillar and birth to the butterfly, and there's pain in that. Many people say, "I tried to do that, but it didn't work." No, it was working; if you're feeling stressed and painful that means you're letting go.

When I talk about the fact that being is the most important thing, often people will say things like "I'd love to do this, but how can I just be when I've got a job and bills to pay?" or "How am I going to solve my problems without worrying about them?" If you had a thought like that, realize that the exact reason that you gave for why you can't connect to the moment is the actual reason that you have to. What you can't see from where you are is that when we finally take that leap, allow ourselves to be, and truly surrender, there is an infinite number of ideas that will support us better than the highest-paying stagnant job that doesn't excite us. In that place of connection are the answers to all of the problems that you've allowed your ego to create in your life. Many times those problems are solved immediately as you enter that space of knowing and realize that your problem is actually just an illusion.

So you can stay in that job or situation that doesn't fulfill you, but realize that each moment you sacrifice your connection to yourself, and listen to the doubt and fear in your mind, takes you one step closer to being the ice cube. When you make the fear of your mind real and do what it says to do, you make the illusion of separation that your mind has created real too, and you cut yourself off from the possibility of the ocean. Taking a leap like quitting a job you hate or leaving a relationship that feels heavy can be scary because the mind's protection mechanism wants to keep you safe from the unknown, but true fulfillment will never come from the illusion of safety the mind tries to create for you.

Within that illusion of safety, the mind actually makes life much more dangerous for you. It causes the very situations that it is trying to prevent by cutting you off from your connection to yourself. If you work in a job that you hate for your entire life, you're not going to be fulfilled, you're not going to be giving your gift, and life won't be able to express itself through you fully. If you stay in a situation that isn't matching the level of contribution that you can truly give, you're ignoring your gift and are in an argument with your body. When you're not giving your gift, you're not in collaboration with life and you're cut off from your true source of well-being, so it's likely that you're going to get either sick, depressed, or addicted . . . and there go your safety and security.

The safest thing you can do is live on the edge of life and take leaps every day that cause your internal knowing to grow bigger than it was yesterday. Your safety isn't in your retirement fund or your savings account, it's in your ability to listen to your heart and connect to the guidance that is moving you toward opportunities that will give you the real security that the mind has been promising all along.

So like I said, the reasons we tell ourselves that we can't live in the space of total connection to ourselves are actually the reasons that we have to. The next chapter is based around an exercise that will help ingrain that understanding in your body and might completely change the way you see your life. I'll make an effort to be funnier in that chapter too.

chapter 17

This Is a Choose-Your-Own-Adventure Life

I'd like to show you another of the many ways that you can allow yourself to melt. This exercise will give you the opportunity to understand the endless possibility that tapping into your ocean will open up for you. If you do this, it has the potential to help you see how much you've been limiting yourself and show you how to bring a whole new awareness into your life.

I want to just mention how important it is that you actually do this exercise, as well as the other ones that I offer in this book. I can't be personally invested in what you get out of this book, but I do know that you will get so much more from it if you truly invest in yourself and take the time and effort to truly embody the things that you're reading about here. If you just read through this chapter but don't do the exercise, it's kind of like going to the gym and having someone explain to you what running on a treadmill is like without ever actually getting on it. It will give you a really great intellectual understanding of what running on a treadmill is *probably* like, but until you finally step onto it and start running, you won't see any real results in your life. Sometimes hearing this kind of information is just enough to get people excited and feeling really good, thinking about all of the possibilities in their life, but often that feeling of contentment creates just enough relief to give people an excuse not to take action on what they've learned.

So actually do this.

A lot of times, we're scared to move into this place of being that we've been talking about. We're afraid to let go and melt because we believe that we'll lose something. We believe that we'll lose someone else's love. We believe that if we stop listening to the chaos of our minds, our lives will fall apart. Here's an exercise that you can do that will allow you to remind and prove to yourself what the actual possibilities are when you move into and start acting from that place of being.

So, if you realized that you were dreaming right now and you could do anything that your heart desired, what would you do? Whatever your answer is, you should follow that desire. I truly believe this.

When I say that to people, what usually happens is they say what they want to do but then immediately say why that thing wouldn't work. So if you read the last chapter about melting into the ocean, you might have said something like "I would love to do that . . . but I don't have enough money saved up" or "If I didn't have kids, I'd let myself follow my calling." Many people never understand that they are saying the thing that they actually want to do, but they're more focused on the reasons they think they can't do it. You might want to melt but, because of conditioning, you also might be paying even more attention to why you can't. I understand that those reasons you believe that you can't do something are real on one level, but with this exercise, I want to show you an entirely new dimension where those situations don't stop you from following the calling of your heart. To help you with those objections, here's a way to prove to yourself that you'll be safe. In fact, this exercise won't just show you that you'll be safe if you step more into being, it will show you how safe and supported you are whenever you decide to follow any inspired passion that you'd love to pursue but think you can't.

So for this exercise, what I want you to do is grab a notebook, or two blank pieces of paper, and a pen or a pencil. If you can, use a blank left page and a blank right page in a notebook; that would work great. Basically you want to get two pieces of blank paper side by side and some kind of writing device. Like this:

Also, a situation like this would work too:

You should avoid this though:

That paper would be hard to do this exercise on.

This is the worst option:

That piece of paper has a fish on it. You will not get a lot out of this exercise if you choose a piece of paper with a fish on it. Actually, screw it, I'm just going to put a couple blank pages in this book so you don't mess this up.

Okay, so now that we've got the paper thing sorted out . . .

We have so many insights, ideas, and callings that show up for us every day that we almost don't even notice because we're so used to ignoring them. One of the things that we don't understand is that statements like "Yeah, but I can't because . . ." are just excuses that we use to stay the same. It's almost like whenever we feel something that is expansive and pulling us into something bigger than what we've been before, our minds immediately start to scramble to find some reason to keep us small and in familiar territory. That's just our ice being afraid to melt. Because we've become such masters at swatting these million-dollar ideas away day after day, we end up focusing much more on why we can't do what we really want to do than why we can or why we should.

For this exercise, what I want you to do is take out your pen or pencil and, on the left page, write down all of the things that you would do or want to have in your life if you actually had a magic wand. What are all the things you would do if you didn't have the ability to say, "Yeah, but . . ." or "I can't because . . ."? Write down all of the ways that you would connect to yourself, all of the creative projects you would do, all of the things you want to do with people you love, and all of the things that just excite you any time you think about them. All of the things you write down are actually things that, if you did them, would help your ice cube melt. Even just by acknowledging and writing them down, you're melting a little bit because you are accessing the calling inside of you. These are all things that go beyond the story of limitation your mind has created, so moving toward them would transcend that protective story.

Spend a few minutes and make a list of every inspired idea you can think of. Everything you want to feel. Everything you want to experience. Really let yourself go. Write down like fifty to a hundred things. When you hear that, there might be a part of you going, "Oh, I don't want to do this." That's the "Yeah, but . . ." part of you that is stopping you from growing, the ice cube part of you that is scared to melt. It's trying to stop you from experiencing something that would be death to the ice and would show you how much you've been listening to a voice that is sabotaging your own fulfillment. That pessimistic voice that wants to shoot everything down before you even try it *isn't* helping you, it's stifling you from accessing your true power. I'm acting like it's a given that you don't want to do this exercise; I'm sure most people are actually excited to do this. I'm probably just projecting how much I never want to do the exercises that books tell me to do . . . because sometimes I try to stay ice too, but I'm never fulfilled when I do.

Okay, so do this now . . . write out all the things that you would want to do, feel, have, and experience if you knew anything was possible. Do you want to take a trip somewhere spontaneously? Do you want to spend a week at a cabin and just connect to yourself? Do you want to write a book? Do you want to be more loving to yourself and other people? Do you want to find the perfect mate? Tap into those deepest desires that you've never told anyone about because you're afraid someone might shoot them down. These are your dreams. Make sure that the things you write down are your soul's expansive calling, not the things that you think you *should* write. What does your soul actually want?

Another thing to keep in mind while you're writing is to make sure that you're expressing what you *want*, not what you *don't* want. It's amazing how many times I ask someone what they really want and they say something like "I don't want to be broke anymore." This exercise is about what we're moving toward, not what we're running away from. When you have clarity and confidence in what you're moving toward, you don't have to constantly be looking over your shoulder at what you're trying to avoid.

So, spend a few minutes doing something for yourself that could really change everything as you open up a conversation with your true desires. I'll wait here while you do that. Here's an example of what that might look like:

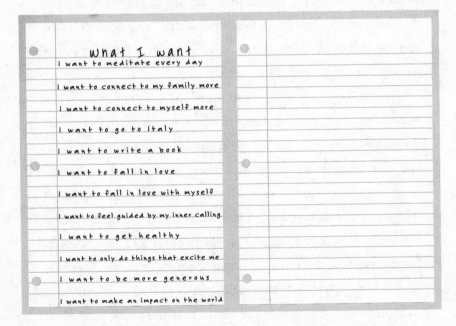

Okay, great, so you did it, right? If you didn't do it, you really shouldn't keep reading until you do, because I'm going to talk about stuff that only the people who did it will get. Hearing this informationally is way different from actually experiencing it. If you keep reading without doing it, it will ruin the surprise if you ever do want to do it. I want you to do this without knowing what I'm about to tell you. So *actually* do this (yes, even you, Michele at Simon & Schuster).

So, for all of you who *definitely* did this exercise, how crazy was that? It's amazing how good it feels to just let ourselves live in a place of possibility for a second.

Now, if you've ever had any of those ideas before and you didn't do them, then that means at some point, you came up with a reason that you couldn't do them. Everything that you wrote on the left-hand page has probably come up before, but it was met with a "Yeah, but I can't do that because . . ." Am I right? If you had on the list that you want to travel more, then you might have said to yourself at some point, "Yeah, but I don't have the money and I can't take time off work." If you have on your list that you want to get in shape, you might have said, "Yeah, but I don't have the time and my family always eats bad food." Whatever the reason, if you haven't been doing the things that you dream about, there's some excuse that your mind has come up with that is stopping you.

What we're going to do now is, on the right page, for everything that you said you would want to do or have, you're going to write down the "Yeah, but . . ." that has been keeping you from doing it. This is ice talk, but you're going to honor it for *one last time* just to do this exercise. So, if on the left side you said, "I want to quit my job," and the reason that you haven't is because you believe you will be broke, write "But I will be broke" on the right side.

So go to that right side now and write down all of the reasons your mind has come up with to keep you from following your true callings. Here's what that should look like now:

What I want	Why I can't
I want to meditate every day	but I don't have enough time
I want to connect to my family more	but they don't understand me
I want to connect to myself more	but I've tried that before
I want to go to Italy	but I don't have the money
I want to write a book	but I don't know how
I want to fall in love	but what if I'm unlovable?
I want to fall in love with myself	but I can't stand myself
I want to feel guided by my inner calling	but I need other peoples advice
I want to get healthy	but it's too hard
I want to only do things that excite me	but I have responsibilities
I want to be more generous	but I don't have enough as it is
I want to make an impact on the world	but who will listen to me?

Okay, done? Cool. I waited a really long time for you to finish that one, but it's fine.

So, first of all, now that you've written that out on both sides, look back at *only* the left side. I want you to notice where you feel each thing you wrote down in your body. I want you to really read these things and pay attention to every part of your body and what type of sensation you feel. Is it exciting? Is it expansive? Where do you feel it? In your stomach? In your entire body? Take a second and read through everything you wrote down on the left side and really tune in to what part of your body is activated by each thing. At the bottom of the left page you can even write down a couple notes and explore everything you felt when you read it.

Done with that?

When I ask my clients to do this, they almost always say that they feel those left-page things somewhere in their chest or in their gut. Sometimes they feel them in their entire body and there is this electric excitement that shoots through them. That's a sign that you're moving toward the ocean. These left-page desires are all ways to melt. These are inspirations that are coming from the whole of your being, and you can feel that when you think about them.

Now I want you to do the same thing with the right side. Look through everything you wrote on the right side and notice where you feel those. Go ahead and do that.

So if you did that on the right side, I'd imagine that for most of them you felt a sensation higher up in your body, probably in either your neck or your head. Or you might have felt a pain somewhere in your body, and that's the body's response to feeling in your head. That's because the reasons you've come up with for why you can't do something come from the limited perspective of your head. They come from your ice, your fear, your survival mechanisms, your old story. Those reasons are mind-based illusions that are only taking into consideration external circumstances and aren't connected to the billions of ways that you could create any of those things in your life.

The more we come up with reasons why we can't do something, the more we cut ourselves off from our bodies and the intelligence of our entire beings. If you looked through any of what you wrote down and you felt something move in your body—if you felt an expansive, excited feeling about any of those things on your left page—realize this: that feeling is a *preview*. That feeling is telling you that if you listen to it and move toward the thing that excites you, you'll feel more of that feeling. It's saying, "When you do this thing, you will always feel this way." And guess what, the more you feel that way, the more you connect to the ocean. The more you connect to the ocean, the more ideas show up. The more ideas show up, the more you feel good and on the edge of your evolution . . . and that's how you start to truly feel fulfilled and in alignment with yourself.

When you look at the right page, notice that you feel most of those fears and doubts in your head. Then realize that when you listen to those reasons why you *can't* do something, you'll get more of *that* feeling. By listening to the voice that keeps you from your calling, you'll shrink into a smaller, contracted version of yourself and start to live within the confines of your ice cube.

I want you to picture a Choose Your Own Adventure book. When I was a kid, we had these books that allowed you to decide what you wanted the characters to do and experience, and at the end of the chapters they would say something like:

If you want to go into the cave, turn to page 72.
If you want to go to the castle, turn to page 68.

So these books would allow you to influence the story and create your own destiny. Life is like a Choose Your Own Adventure book.

Life is always giving us options to either step into our true power or retreat into the "safety" of our ice cube. Now imagine if the book said:

Do you want to take this leap, yes or no?

If you choose no, the book's like, "All right then, thanks for reading, the book's over." The adventure ends when you're not open to the options it gives you. That's what we're doing all day long. We're saying no to all of these opportunities that life keeps handing us, and it can't lead us on the adventure that it has planned unless we take that leap.

I know all of those "Yeah, but . . ." reasons are real things that exist on one level, but one of the things we don't understand is that when we actually act on inspiration and move into that expansive feeling in our bodies, life starts to just serve up endless ways to make that thing a reality. We don't understand that the path will show up as soon as we take that first step. We just have to melt first and move beyond the fears that are keeping us from taking that step.

What I've learned from my experience is, the way to truly move with the flow of life is to look for and move into those expansive feelings that happen in my body. All I ask is "What moves me into my body?" That's how I make every decision. Does it make me feel lighter or heavier? "Do I want to go to the gym, move my body, and connect to myself?" That feels light and allows my ice to melt. "Do I want to hang out and watch Netflix while eating almond butter and pita chips?" That feels heavy and supports the ice. Sometimes it's the opposite. Sometimes going to the gym feels heavy and Netflix feels light. Sometimes, maybe my soul feels like I've gone to the gym too many times because I can't even fit my biceps into my shirt anymore, so it tells me that I need to relax and just watch *Roseanne* for a minute.

It's not about the thing, it's about honoring what *you* feel in the moment. The more and more I learn to trust that light feeling I experience in my body, the more I'm able to make effortless decisions based on my actual guidance instead of the addictive desires of my mind.

We've trained ourselves to go after what feels heavier—that's your right page. You've trained yourself to stay in your head and ignore the calling that's coming through in your body. It's like the example we used before of not using the elevator in the office you've worked in for forty years. That elevator goes to other floors and on other floors life is easier, but if you've trained yourself your entire life to never go into the elevator, you need to come up with reasons why you haven't been using it. Because, at some level, you know in your heart it would be easier to take the elevator, you have to create all of these "Yeah, but . . ." excuses to justify why you don't use it. Eventually, you just think that life is all about coming up with reasons why you don't do what you really want to do. We've become artists at creating brilliant ways to stop ourselves from stepping into our greatness. That's what we've used our creativity for, up until now. We've used it so frequently that it's second nature to us; we don't even know we do it.

Now here's the craziest thing . . . notice how many of the things on the right page, on the "Yeah, but . . ." page, could actually be the reason why you have to do the thing on the left page. You might have something on the left page like "I want to live in my calling" and on the right page you have a reason you can't like "Yeah, but I have kids to take care of." That's one of the biggest reasons that you *should* live in your calling, because you can give your kids permission to do the same and be an example of the fact that they can do anything too.

Or you might have said, "I want to go away for a month and write a book," and then said, on the right page, "But I can't because I don't have any money." That's all the more reason to go live in your calling, because what you might not understand is, in your calling, you're going to step into a new dimension and create a confidence that can come up with creative content that will bring you so much more abundance and fulfillment than staying where you are and listening to your right page. But you can't see this until you honor the left page. The delay of the decision to follow your heart is where your pain is. It has nothing to do with what you're about to do, it has to do with making the choice. You'll never know the exact details of why you need to make the leap *until* you actually do it. If you're looking at both pages and trying to see what life will be like after you leap, that will never work.

This world has trained itself to live on the right page and ignore its calling. That's the way people stay ice. You wrote out your calling on the left page, so if you want to become the ocean and allow your ice to melt, *start* doing the things on the left page and *stop* listening to the reasons on the right page. As you do that you will go to new levels in your life that will take care of all of the "Yeah, but . . ."s that your mind comes up with.

I have gotten so much proof that every time I feel a calling to make a leap, it's taking me to an entirely new and exciting place that will bring me more fulfillment and closer to the truth of what I am. Like everyone else, I have a part of me that says, "I want to do this . . . ," and then my mind comes up with a "Yeah, but . . .". Every time that happens, I just step back and look at those two versions of myself and go, "Now which version do I want to step into?" If I step into the opportunity, the fear leaves, because I trust that feeling more than what my mind is shouting at me. If I believe the fear and listen to the reasons why I can't, I cut off the opportunity. I know I said that before, but now that you've done this exercise, I think you have more of an experiential understanding of what I mean by that.

If you really understand that, any time you have a decision to make, you'll feel either excited in your body or scared and in your head, so just ask yourself, "Which would I rather live in?" Whatever decision you make will move you toward that reality. "I really want to do this. Yeah, but I can't afford it." Well, maybe you'll be able to afford it when you decide to do it. This sounds crazy to a lot of people; that's their "Yeah, but . . ." brain that they've trained themselves to listen to.

I have made so many leaps in my life. So many crazy, crazy leaps. Everything I'm talking about here has proven, for me, to be 100 percent true.

A year ago, we were doing an event at a two-hundred-seat theater, and my teammate Dan said, "What do you really want to do?" Immediately I said, "I want to do a huge theater . . . like a two thousand seater." Right when I said that, I could feel this insane excitement in my body, but my mind said, "Yeah, but we could barely fill a two hundred seater." THAT'S WHY I NEEDED TO DO IT. I needed an excitement to pull my creativity and inner alignment into a place that was way beyond the icy stagnancy I was feeling in these smaller events. Believe it or not, when we said yes to doing a huge theater, it ended up being *easier* to fill because the excitement we had about it helped us access the entire ocean of possibilities available to us. We were immediately inspired to create all of these new videos that ended up getting millions and millions of views and filled the event within a couple of weeks.

The excited feeling we had about taking that leap didn't contain any of the information about how we were going to fill the theater, or the fact that it would bring in hundreds of thousands of new followers, or that it would bring in a book deal, or any of other the things that have come after it. Can you believe that? This book is actually being written because of that one day when I decided to step into what I actually wanted to do and move out of the limitations of my ice cube. I had no idea this book that I'm writing right now would be a part of that decision. Also, I wouldn't have known many of the things that I'm writing about in this book if I hadn't leapt into the alignment to fill that two thousand seater. By doing that I accessed so much more of my ocean, became even more connected to myself, and learned what I needed to learn to be able to write this book. And by writing this book, which was also scary to me at one point, I'm accessing even more of that ocean and swimming deeper and deeper. I couldn't see any of that before I leapt, but I could *feel it*. The second we said, "Let's do it," the fear dissolved and opened up the possibility for all of those creative ideas to come in.

I have a lifetime of examples of how when you live in your left page, the right page goes away. If you live in the right page, your left page goes away. So, look at your list and if you want to change your life, start doing as many of the left-page things as you can, because then you are actually having faith. You're not just talking about God and the universe all the time and not listening to the calling. That feeling is the calling. That's what faith is. That feeling is saying, "Do it." So do it, because you will CHANGE THE WORLD if you listen to your left page.

chapter 18

Okay Everyone, Back Up, I'm Gonna Prove That We're All One

The exercise in the last chapter was an amazing way to help prove to yourself how much the illusion of your limited story keeps you from following the guidance of your heart. From that, an awareness might be starting to show up in you, where you're almost just watching those types of limiting thoughts appear in your mind without believing or being owned by them quite as much as before. That is an amazing sign that you are starting to melt.

The change that you're having is so profound that you might not even notice that it's happening. What I mean by that is, the part of you that compares yourself to other people and your past is starting to fall away. The self-monitor that sees itself as a separate story is dying, so you're probably not looking to your past as much for signs that you're shifting. Everyone started this book at a different level of awareness, but if you've been reading with an open heart, you are likely in an entirely different place than you were when you began.

Before we become aware of the illusions we've been caught in, we're like a baby chick that is still in its shell. This stage is when you believe that your entire life is your circumstances and past story. When you're in the shell, you are only your accomplishments, and your worthiness is totally dependent on what other people think of you. This stage is really stressful because you're constantly spinning plates and trying to control your circumstances so you can protect your story and who you think you are. You only recognize who you are as the fear of not getting love from your parents, even though you don't know that's the case. In this stage you think that life *is* the shell, and the illusion of your identity will do everything it can to keep it from breaking.

Being stuck in the shell totally serves a purpose. You would never pull a baby chick out of its shell before it was ready to hatch; it wouldn't be able to survive. You can't force anyone out of the shell until they're ready. This is like trying to pop a balloon before it's fully inflated.

The second stage is when there's a crack in your shell and you're actually ready to start hatching. This is where maybe something happened that broke your story and a little bit of that illusion dissolved for a second. You catch a glimpse that there's something more outside of your story, but because you're mainly still living inside the illusion, the crack is really scary. Even though the mind is terrified of the crack, you've had some sort of awakening that knows you're more than just the shell. There's not a human being that is reading this book that hasn't at least gotten to the "crack in the shell" phase. If your shell didn't already have a crack, this book would just make you angry because your mind would feel threatened.

What this book is doing is just opening that crack more. It's giving you, and me, permission to trust that instinct in us that knows there's something beyond what we've seen.

The third stage is getting outside of the shell. There's a very good chance that, by now, you're almost completely out of the shell. You know you're out of the shell if you can look at the illusion of your identity and understand that it's almost like a character in a video game, and you're the one playing the game. This stage is the process of stepping outside of your story and realizing that nothing in this world can actually hurt you, it can only hurt the illusion that your mind has created of you. As you leave the shell, you start moving from your head to your heart.

We can use a version of the graph that we used in chapter seven to represent these different stages . . .

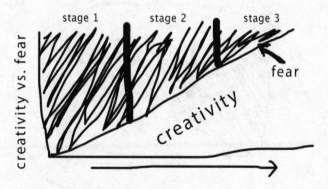

This chapter will help you move through these stages and pull your awareness out of the shell even more, and it could possibly take you all the way to the fourth stage, where aliens from the planet Zarglom will recognize your ascension and beam you to their home planet, where you'll live forever in a house made of diamond dust.

That's not actually the fourth stage, but that will probably be the paragraph newspapers quote when they do book reviews. The real fourth stage is when you realize that the shell was just a figment of your own imagination. This is where you realize that you are all of this, and that the illusion of separation was just something you created so that you could rediscover yourself again in a new way. This is where you identify with your infinite nature and know that you are creation itself. This is where you actually melt into the ocean and see that we're not just all connected, we're all the exact same thing.

Stage four is where you realize you're the entire graph. You're the arrow and the squiggly lines. You created the process. You're all of it.

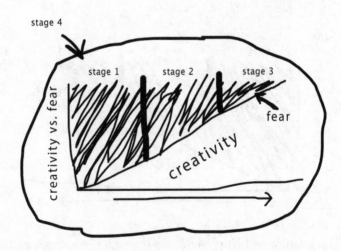

So now that this space is starting to open up within you, I want to share one of the most impactful things that I do in my life to allow this melting process to happen. This isn't really something that you're going to do, it's more something that's going to do you.

(Not in a sexual way. It's not like that time when I lost my virginity and then told my mom about it within seven minutes. This exercise is not me losing my virginity again. Jesus, this book is weird.) It's really on a completely different level than the last exercise. If that last exercise was like baking your ice cube at 350 degrees, this next exercise is like landing on the surface of the sun. That's actually a scientifically proven comparison. You probably already know that if you've seen Albert Einstein's recent Facebook post about it:

Albert Einstein
9 hrs ·

Because I am still alive, I'd like to share my most recent hypothesis:

If Kyle Cease's left and right page exercise is equal to baking your ice cube at 350 degrees, the very next exercise he presents shall be of equal proportion to landing on the surface of the sun.

—Albert Einstein (alive)

Like   Comment   Share

1.2m   Top Comments

107,950 shares

Write a comment...

Grimel Griln I've never thought of it this way Albert... like most, I've typically compared Kyle's next exercise to that of a microwave on full power. Thank you for your enlightening perspective.
Like · Reply · 73 · 5 hrs
↳ 26 Replies

Garyll Gorgenhop Hate to disagree, but this just is not accurate. Kyle Cease's next exercise has neither the velocity, nor the integrated mass to be a suitable comparison to landing on the sun.
Like · Reply · 11 · 7 hrs

Scran Grn Garyll Gorgenhop, maybe if you took into account the rotational gravity acceleration of the earth you wouldn't be so confused. I think you owe Albert (who is still alive) an apology you troll.
Like · Reply · 32 · 9 hrs
↳ 3 Replies · 6 hrs

Earlier in the book, I said I would talk more about meditation. Guess what time it is?

Pretty much every day, I wake up and just sit for a while and connect with myself. That's it. I just sit and watch all of these thoughts that my mind comes up with and connect with the space that all of this is happening in. I just connect to what is real. I *guess* you could call what I do meditation, but like the word "God," I usually don't call it that because everyone has a different perception of what it means and sometimes the concept gets in the way of the experience. This isn't about the technique or the method, it's about giving yourself the time to let your own personal evolution take place, however that might happen for you. There really is no right way to do this. If you're asking, "How do I do this right?" you're making the method more important than you are.

So I just sit. I pick a comfortable position, usually in a chair or at the head of my bed, but I don't have anything specific that I do with my hands and I don't need to be wearing beads or anything. I do make sure that I'm not lying down and that my head isn't resting on anything though, so I don't fall asleep. I also put my phone on airplane mode and set a timer so I don't have to worry about being interrupted or keeping track of time. I then wait for the sauce to boil and add the noodles.

Kyle's Fun Time Question Quiz

Which of the last sentences doesn't belong in the paragraph above and is actually part of a recipe for vegetable pad thai?

A. I also put my phone on airplane mode and set a timer so I don't have to worry about being interrupted or keeping track of time.

B. I do make sure that I'm not lying down and that my head isn't resting on anything though, so I don't fall asleep.

C. I then wait for the sauce to boil and add the noodles.

D. Letter D is not the right answer.

The answer to Kyle's Fun Time Question Quiz is on page 202.

Seriously though, this isn't a big deal, I just sit like a human being with my eyes closed and watch everything that's happening inside. Really, I'm not even watching what's happening. I'm just relaxing into what I am and falling into truth.

It's crazy that this is something that we have to learn to do. For some reason, people think that it's weird or extreme to just spend time sitting with your eyes closed. It's really bizarre that it's much more normal and accepted to scroll through Facebook or watch people pretend to be other people on TV for hours at a time than it is to just sit quietly and connect to yourself for a second. This is actually the most natural thing we can do. It doesn't take any effort at all. I imagine that this is the way that a tree feels. It's always just effortlessly growing into what it's supposed to become.

While the amount of time doesn't really matter, I'll often do this for an hour or two, and as soon as I close my eyes, my mind goes a little crazy. It's absolutely horrified that I've decided to just sit quietly in my bedroom for a while. It's insane. It's like my mind is afraid of being found out that it's a total fraud (maybe that's because it is).

So I make a deal with myself and decide to just sit there for a certain amount of time, and as soon as I close my eyes, my mind starts to come up with all these reasons why this is stupid. It'll say things like "You can't do this for an entire hour, are you crazy?" or "This is so dumb, we're not getting anything done." It'll even say, "We don't have time to do this," even though later it will try to convince me that we have plenty of time to watch multiple episodes of *Roseanne*. It's amazing how much we think that we don't have time for something that could actually change our lives, and then how much time we waste all day doing things that don't fulfill us.

Strangely, on the days that I do this, I actually have *more* time than the days that I don't. Even though this isn't about the results, on the days that I spend an hour or two connecting with myself, I'm more able to tap into a flow that allows me to create on an entirely different level. I literally don't have the time to *not* do this.

When I'm in the illusion of my past story, I believe that I'm less worthy than I am in this moment. As I sit and connect to what I am in this moment, I step out of that story and my alignment raises. When I create this self-connection, I have so much more clarity on whether things feel heavy or light, so instead of taking on things during the day that might be addictive or people-pleasing, I'm more able to trust my calling and move toward what excites me.

Over the last year, I have actually been doing a personal challenge where I've been doing this for two hours a day and then posting a video about it. Since starting that, everything in my life has changed. My presence, my health, my impact, and my abundance have all gone through the roof. Often ideas come directly out of meditation that are so much more beneficial than what I would have been doing otherwise. I can't tell you how many ideas for sketches, new directions for our business, and inspired concepts have come out of this space of total connection to what I truly am. I don't do it for any of those things; I do it because it just feels good to connect to what I truly am. When you take time to connect to yourself, the unlimited creativity that we are all made of just starts to seep into your life and transform everything you do. When you start doing this, you almost can't tell *how* you've changed, because *everything* has changed.

Another benefit from this is that, for the first time, I've been able to experience connection *and* freedom at the same time. My entire life, those two things have been opposing concepts. It always felt like I was either in a relationship and feeling connection while sacrificing freedom, or I was single feeling freedom while sacrificing connection. Through the process of this exercise, not only do I now feel both of those things at the same time, but I actually feel a deeper connection than I've ever had in any relationship and more freedom than I've ever had in any singleness. Pretty sure "singleness" is not a word, but spell check isn't underlining it with a red squiggly line, so I'm gonna go with it. Hold on, I'm gonna Google it to see if it's actually a word or not. Holy shit, it's a word. What a stupid-sounding word. That's the kind of word an *idiot would have on his luggage*. (What movie is that from? The answer is also on page 202.)

So anyway, right when you sit down, tons of thoughts might show up trying to get you to give up. No matter what comes up, be okay with it and stay there. That's the most important thing. There's nothing stopping you from just staying there. The decision to stay in your truth instead of listening to the thoughts that are trying to pull you back into the illusion has the power to CHANGE WORLDS. We already know that these thoughts aren't real and that they are just trying to keep you in the shell, so this isn't about controlling the thoughts or trying to make them go away, because that would put you in resistance to them and give them power. Instead, we just allow them to be, completely. This is much more about connecting to the space that all of these thoughts show up in than it is about stopping thoughts. We're not trying to do that at all.

As you just sit in silence and keep going deeper, you'll start to feel how much those thoughts don't even matter. As you just watch from the awareness in you that never changes and notice how everything else comes and goes, you start to experience this perspective that knows everything is perfect exactly the way it is. You stop fighting against anything. You find out that nothing is wrong and that in this moment, you are totally whole and complete. Thoughts might come up to convince you otherwise, but as you allow those thoughts to be exactly as they are and notice the part of you that has no objection to the moment, the walls start to dissolve and there is an expansion that happens in your body.

The mind loves to convince us that one thing is better than another, that life is better than death, that happiness is better than sadness, that a sunny day is better than a rainy day. By having a preference for anything, you create a resistance to its perceived opposite, and this is where your pain truly comes from. When you allow your awareness to step out of the illusion, you move beyond preference and into a space that is in total appreciation for everything, even the things you once saw as problems or challenges.

We are not here to judge the world outside and try to change it to fit our minds' controlling, limited viewpoint. Instead we are here to see the love in everything. Everything is you. Everything is in purpose. Even your thinking that you are out of purpose is in purpose.

Your pain is in your love for some of life but not all of it. Our resistance to *what is* cuts us off from our soul. Our acceptance of *what is* connects us to everything and makes way for a true internal healing followed by an external healing. As your internal state becomes fluid and in alignment with your true nature, your external world will begin to mirror that alignment. Later you will discover internal and external *are the same*.

As we sit and watch, we can discover that the judgments that come up in our heads are, and always have been, an illusion. All of our separation and fear is pure illusion. You will start to discover that the only difference between you and everyone else is the story in your head. This sounds crazy to the mind because it is a separation machine. For the mind to survive it has to be separate from everything and everyone it sees so it can maintain its individual story. When we move beyond the mind, we enter a dimension where we see how much of a lie that actually is. Our bodies and minds are like individual rivers that all flow to and from the same ocean.

So guess what? You are reading a book that *you* wrote. You are me. The only thing that separates us is the illusion of the mind telling you that I am my body, gender, race, past story, nationality, etc. But I am you. I am writing from the same place that connects to your core.

This photo was taken by Alannah Avelin, who is also me.

So do you understand that this is you? The only thing that separates you is your mind, but if you get out of your mind and you just look into my eyes, you'll realize that you're looking into your own eyes . . . and they're gorgeous.

Your mind might say, "No, you're different from me . . . ," but the only examples that it can come up with for why we are different are external things. My skin color, my gender, my history, my past. Try proving that we're different without something that comes from your story. You can't. Notice that when you try to find reasons that we're different, you have to use your mind. Beyond our stories, we're the same. The only thing that can try to disprove that is your mind, and we've disproved the mind throughout this entire book. The mind's separating, fear-based perspective isn't the truth. But that's totally okay; we were never meant to rely on the mind for our ultimate truth.

So your job is really simple, if you want to do this and experience connection on an entirely new level. All you have to do is just sit and stay there as all of these things come up that might want to distract you, or cause you pain, or tell you that you're crazy, or that you're unworthy, or that you're unlovable, or whatever. All you have to do is sit there in the face of that illusion and allow your ocean to meet it.

No matter what you do when you sit and close your eyes, you're always evolving. You're always getting closer to yourself, no matter if it feels painful, or joyous, or scary, or boring. Whatever story you might attach to it, you're evolving. One moment you'll feel contracted, then all of a sudden that pain will break away and you'll feel expansive. Then a new pain will come and take its place, and then *that* will break away. Even when you're in pain, notice how there's still a perspective beyond it that is totally okay. That's the truth of what you are, and as you keep feeling the pain and contrast, while also noticing that other perspective, you will continually slip more and more into that perspective that is totally safe, or as we called it before, *deep down*.

The more you connect to everything, the more you start to realize that you are your head, you are your heart, you are the book you're reading, you are the author who wrote it, you're everything. You're the designer of this whole play that is here to lead you back to what you truly are and to allow you to experience yourself fully.

If you decide right now that it's more important to you to know the truth and experience actual freedom than to live in the addiction of your mind, do this one thing. Just sit and let the old illusions of your past story crumble as you discover the depth of what you are truly capable of experiencing in this world. Sometimes you'll get entangled in that story and sometimes you won't, but the most important thing is that you are the process, not the end goal. The more you do this, the more you'll connect to the journey of your life and the less you'll be addicted to the results.

When you sit with your eyes closed and just be, while your mind unravels and falls apart, all of that separation dissolves and the only thing left is total connection to all of life. When you are one with everything, your pain truly dissolves, and you create a giant portal for all of your old stories to leave through. Your embracing and acceptance of everything, including your darkest fears, is where you will discover a light that has never been seen before. You are love. Period.

Before you start the next chapter, I invite you to get away from everything, put your phone on airplane mode, set a timer for an hour or so, close your eyes, and do this. Actually do this. Tapping into this space before you read the rest of the book will make this whole thing start moving so much faster.

The first day of doing this is like going to the gym for the first time. When you start going to the gym, you start a process that you know will take time and commitment; you don't expect to lose a hundred pounds on day one. This is the same thing. I always say to people, "Don't knock it until you've tried it for at least ninety days continuously." Don't try to check whether this is working or not until you've done it for at least ninety days.

If you decide to do this for an hour a day for a couple of months, when you look back, I know that you'll notice less fear, more fulfillment, and a connection you had no idea existed. You will find less divisiveness and protection and feel more freedom in your body. Doing this is a heroic act. Your *actually* spending time discovering who you are and stepping into love instead of fear is the thing that will truly shift this planet. So join me and commit to allowing yourself the opportunity to **evolve into the love that you are.**

chapter 19

Now I'm Going to Prove Death Isn't Real . . . Your Other Books Are Shitty

As you can tell by the name of this chapter, we're going to be learning how to create a fun vision board to attract everything you want! Here's one that I made for this book before I knew about copyright issues:

Okay, now make one for you.

Wasn't that fun? Great, now let's talk about death!

In the last chapter, there was a sentence that said, "The mind loves to convince us that one thing is better than another, that life is better than death, that happiness is better than sadness, that a sunny day is better than a rainy day." You might be able to wrap your head around a sunny day being just as good as a rainy day, or sadness's being just as enjoyable as happiness in some way, but the concept that death isn't necessarily worse than life is total insanity to the mind. I'm not talking about the afterlife or heaven or anything like that, I'm just talking about the mental judgment we have around life versus death. To the mind, there is nothing worse than death. It has decided that death is the enemy and that staying alive is its number one job (in fact, that's really its *only* job when it comes down to it).

Many of you are probably thinking, "Of course I'd rather live than die." I get that. We all want to live; that's one of our basic instincts as human beings. However, it's our judgment that death is worse than life, and that death is something to be afraid of, that is the real cause of most of our limiting and fear-based beliefs. Our fear of death is actually the thing that keeps us from truly living.

I want to start off by telling you that I don't know for sure what happens when you die. I've never died, at least not that I know of. I'm also not trying to challenge any religious beliefs or anything like that, and I totally honor everyone's perspective. I'm just sharing some of the insights that I've experienced as I've moved beyond many of the limiting beliefs that I once thought were 100 percent true. This chapter isn't really about uncovering the mystery of death and where we go, or how many mansions or virgins we get when we die, it's more about looking at death as an example of the limitations and fear we create by believing everything our minds tell us. I mean, if you think about it, when you believe that you are just this physical body and mind, death is the ultimate limitation, right?

Take a look at this drawing. I probably didn't need to say that. You'd see it anyway; it's right here.

First, realize that this stick figure is literally the best picture of a human that I can draw. Now, imagine that this stick figure is an actual living person thinking about their existence from their mind's point of view. When we're using our minds to tell us who we are, we are thinking linearly and can only see that our lives begin when we're born, and they end when we die. But if you think about it, the only reason we believe that our lives begin when we're born is that we don't remember anything before it. I don't remember how many scoops of almond butter I ate last night, but that doesn't mean I didn't eat them. I wish it did, but it doesn't.

What I'm getting at is, our minds have created a belief about life and death that is based only on what they have seen and assumed from stories they have heard (from other minds). So, if we're starting to understand that we can't just be the story that our minds have created, maybe what we truly are is also beyond the boundaries of life and death that the mind has created. Even our perspective on life and death, the most foundational belief that we have, is based on the logic of a limited viewpoint. When we begin moving past the limitations of our minds and connecting to the awareness that all of our thoughts, feelings, emotions, and experiences arise in, we realize that our true natures are even beyond what we understand as life and death.

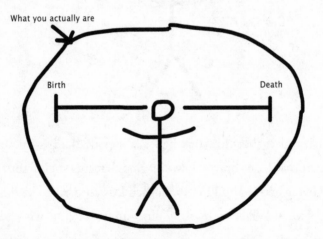

The rest of this book will probably just be me drawing diagrams and then circling them.

Imagine if the second you were born, you were immediately

playing *Super Mario Bros.*, the video game. Imagine that you've had the controller in your hand since birth and you've got a visor on so that the game is the only thing you can see. Pretend there are other people playing the game too, but you know them only through their characters on the screen. You don't know that there's actually someone controlling them, sitting right next to you. If you stayed playing the game for the next thirty years, you would be totally convinced that *Super Mario Bros.* was real life and you would think that you were Mario, this two-dimensional Italian plumber who is fighting turtles. That would be all you ever knew.

If the dude playing Luigi suddenly stopped playing and walked away from the game, Luigi would stop moving on the screen and you would think Luigi was dead. You would mourn Luigi and be so sad, even though he was actually fine. It would just be his character that was gone. After you created the belief that Luigi was dead, the game would seem much scarier, because now you'd be afraid it would end, and you wouldn't know what happened when it ended. Our minds are terrified of the unknown. If you just took your eyes off the screen for a second, you would notice the guy who was playing Luigi was fine, he was just taking a break. You'd probably also notice that there were no turtles trying to kill you outside of the game. You'd probably also have much more fun when you went back to playing *Super Mario Bros.*, now that you knew it wasn't all there was.

As I've been meditating and connecting to the truth underneath all of these fearful thoughts that my mind has created, I've started to see that even the limitations it has created around life and death are just illusions. I guess at this point, I can really only say that they *seem* like illusions, since I'm not writing this after I've been dead, but there is definitely an awareness coming in that is showing me there is an entire other dimension of myself just lovingly watching my character do its thing, that isn't afraid of dying at all. I know this might sound crazy to anyone who hasn't experienced it, but as you more and more begin to disprove all the little things that your mind is telling you, it makes you realize that the entire foundation that our belief system is built on is faulty.

Could you imagine what life would be like if we weren't afraid of dying? Everything would change. I don't mean that everyone would be skydiving to work. I just mean that almost all of our fears and limitations would dissolve in the knowing that whatever happens, we're going to be okay. We're just playing a game.

As I said earlier in the book, all of the fear that we experience is really directly associated with our fear of death. When we're worried about money, we're in survival mode and scared that we're going to die, at least on some level. Your mind immediately takes the thought "I don't have enough money" and then reminds you that you need money for food and shelter, and if you don't have money for food and shelter, you'll die.

Even our fear of not being loved or given attention is related to death, because that's what would happen if our parents didn't show us love and take care of us. That's why we learn all of those behaviors to get love and approval from others. Every single fear that we have is a protection mechanism that the mind has created to keep us alive. Unfortunately, it's that primal, unconscious fear of death that motivates many of the fear-based actions that cause so much suffering on this planet.

If you're scared to die, then really, that just means you have a thought that you're in resistance to—the thought of death. We think of the fear of death as more real than any other fear we experience, but at this point, since we don't know what happens when you die, the fear of death is really just like any other thought we've created and attached meaning to. It's like being afraid of a dark hallway in an old hotel. Because you don't know what's at the end of that hallway, your mind comes up with a bunch of horrible possibilities to keep you out of potential danger, but there could be a huge trampoline with a cotton-candy version of Jennifer Aniston on it waiting for you with all the Taco Time you need at the end of it, for all you know. If you're in resistance to the idea your mind has created of death, you're fighting against it and adding stress to your life . . . which ironically will speed up your death.

As we know, our minds falsely link all types of meanings to things that happen in our lives to keep us safe. When I was a kid, I was bitten by a dog when I was walking down a street in Seattle. It sucked. Twenty years later, when I walked down that same street again, my mind brought up all this fear and anxiety because it believed that what happened before was going to happen again. So it falsely linked the pain of being attacked by a dog to that street.

This is how our minds work. If you get in a relationship with someone who cheats on you, your mind might think, "Every relationship will end this same way, so now I have to put this guard up and be suspicious of anyone I'm in a relationship with." Your mind doesn't understand that it's taking the trauma it experienced once and thinking that it will happen over and over again. So you're trying to save your life all the time because your mind has falsely linked everything together.

When you start to observe those types of fears long enough and realize that they are just illusions, you start to see all of it from this limitless, loving space that truly has no fear of anything. The longer I sit and just observe all of that and realize how crazy and off-base the mind is, the more I become connected to that limitless space, instead of this fearful mind that is always trying to scare me out of doing everything. We have the opportunity to move our awareness out of the small, limited person and into the space of love surrounding that person at any time. You are constantly choosing to put your attention on either the character in the game or the person playing the game.

When you can connect to the whole thing, the fears and worries of the limited story you've been identifying with aren't such a big deal anymore. Imagine that, after you became aware that *Super Mario Bros.* is just a game, when Mario is about to go up to a castle, a little thought bubble popped up and said, "I'm scared, I don't want to." As the person controlling Mario, that thought bubble saying Mario is scared wouldn't really affect you. It wouldn't make you afraid to go into the castle. You also wouldn't get into an argument with the thought bubble. You'd just know that you were going to be fine and go into the castle anyway.

This is exactly what happens when we start to realize that we're actually the awareness behind this limited story of a person that our minds have created. All of the fears, doubts, insecurities, guilt, shame, and worries of the mind are just like thought bubbles on the screen of a video game. We can see them pop up in the mind, but we don't have to believe or fight against them. We just rest in this space of total connection to our truth and move based on our inspiration, instead of the fear of our character.

In this limitless space, there aren't any labels anymore. This awareness doesn't see good vs. bad or anything like that. This is the point of view that doesn't see death as something to be afraid of. This is going to sound weird, but in a way, that limitless space *is* death. What I've been experiencing in meditation, after clearing out a lot of limitation-based thoughts, is that I'm touching a place that is not only beyond life and death, but a place that is actually both life and death at the same time. It's the space that allows even the concept of life and death to arise. This is some deep shit.

How do I know this? I don't. Honestly, this is just a feeling of awareness and oneness that I get as I move beyond the limited story of myself more and more. As I speak, or in this case write, I'm constantly just moving toward what feels like truth in my body, and I can tell you, this feels like the deepest truth I have experienced. There's a feeling of total expansion and freedom in this space that completely transcends the mind's perspective on where life begins and ends.

Nothing here is something that I am trying to convince you of, but I can say that, in this awareness, there is the opportunity for freedom from the trauma, the fear, the suffering, and the despair that our minds create around the story of survival we have been told. That fearful perspective isn't wrong, but it's just a perspective from one level of our being. As we embrace the entirety of what we are, that limiting perspective will start to loosen and be seen through as we access our eternal natures.

This life is a beautiful experience, and even being lost in the story of the mind is amazing and beneficial from a universal perspective. However, it feels to me as if there is a pull toward our evolving out of the limited perspective of the mind that causes so much suffering in our world. As we enter into this new awareness, every aspect of our society will move toward connection instead of separation, collaboration instead of competition, compassion instead of condemnation. When we know that we aren't the body, or the mind, or our possessions, or our achievements, we will be able to give and receive in harmony with life and tap into a level of creativity, joy, and fulfillment that has yet to be experienced on this planet.

ANSWERS FROM EARLIER IN THE BOOK:

1. C, "I then wait for the sauce to boil and add the noodles."
2. *Spaceballs.*

If you close your eyes and sit with this, notice that there is one perspective or point of focus that feels smaller and in your head, somewhere around where your eyes are. Then notice that there is a larger awareness that surrounds that small perspective. It might even feel like it is behind or above you. Don't try to move your attention there with your mind, just notice that it's there; it will pull you there on its own.

This awareness is always there. It might seem like it's not there sometimes, but that's only because, in those moments, you've chosen to be focused in the perspective of the mind, believing everything it tells you. Notice how, from that larger perspective, the thoughts of your mind might still be there, but they feel more distant and maybe more insignificant. From this perspective, you can start to see the holes in the logic of the mind and you can see situations from all angles.

This is an awareness that crept up on me after years of transformation and tons of meditation, so if it's not something that you experience right away, that's okay. I'm not even saying that this is something that everyone will experience in the same way. What I know is, we each have the ability and opportunity in this life to move more into the fullness of our being. Whether or not what I'm sharing here helps you to do that isn't up to me. The only thing I can do is share what I'm being called to share and release myself from the outcome. This is just an invitation to explore yourself even more. Challenge yourself to investigate all of the beliefs that your mind has created, and see if there is another perspective, beyond the mind, that might offer you even more freedom.

You might have to read this chapter more than once for it to make sense. LOL.

I dare you to sit and close your eyes for an hour and a half before you read the next chapter.

chapter 20

Okay, Now You Can Start Asking How Again

Well, I guess now that we're not afraid of dying anymore, we should do some stuff. Seriously though, this is a big point. Really realize that the sky's the limit once you've removed the type of judgment and limitations that the instinctual fear of death makes you have. For many people, almost everything they do is based on this survival instinct telling them to make sure they are safe and protected. It creates a mentality that is just about getting as much as possible, which causes them to be completely cut off from the whole. In this new awareness, we're able to step out of fear and start to take action from a place of being and connection that supplies us with everything we need to create on an entirely new level. Basically, we've struck oil. So now what do we do with it?

This place of being that we've entered, in some ways, *is* the end point. For us to get to that place is really the ultimate goal of this book, if there is such a thing. Moving out of the illusion that we are limited to the thoughts, the emotions, and the story that we've identified with our entire lives is the most important thing we can possibly do. This feeling of freedom is all we're ever looking for when we're searching for something externally. Everything we do from a place other than being is just an attempt to find relief from the mind's telling us we are incomplete. All we want is to connect to the knowing inside of us. All we want is to feel like everything is okay. Without that understanding as our foundation, every action we take will stem from that egoic illusion and we'll always be just one step away from actual fulfillment. So, finding that place of connection and pure being is *always* the answer to *everything*.

So, if this place of being is the finish line, then there's no point for the rest of this book, right? Kind of. The truth is, though, there's actually so much more to talk about. Yes, this place of being is the goal on an *internal* level, but I don't think that we came into this experience as humans *just* for an internal experience. Instead of just meditating into oneness all day, let's do something with the knowing that we are just love and that no matter what we do, everything will be fine. The other half of the journey, to me, is taking this understanding, walking through the doorway of this unlimited creativity we've discovered, and bringing that creativity into the world. Now that we've unhooked ourselves from the weights we've been carrying our entire lives, we can use this understanding as a launchpad to inspire an even fuller expression of ourselves. There's so much imagery in this paragraph, and I'm really proud of it, so I asked a friend to make some artwork for it.

My dear friend, Heather Smith, painted this amazing work of art.

That was an idea in my head, then it was a paragraph, now it's art. This is how life works. When we become a space bigger than our addictive habits and move toward even the smallest idea that excites us, new results that we never could have anticipated start to show up everywhere.

Like I've said many times before, life is a playground. Now that we're in a place of being and letting go of our fear-based minds, we can actually start to see the truth in that statement. There's a reason that when we were kids we just loved to create and were totally enamored of the world around us. We were laughing and playing all day because we didn't have this heavy ego filled with a lifetime of painful past stories. Now that we're moving beyond those past stories, we can start to go back into that pure, childlike state of creativity and start to express ourselves and contribute to the world in a new and even more powerful way.

You can think of the illusion of your past story and your mind as this ball of hair that has been clogging up your ability to connect with the pipeline of infinite possibilities that life has for you. This book has been like a plumber. This book is like Mario! Mario has totally pulled the hair out of your drain, and now your creativity and connection are ready to flow like crazy. You might be thinking, "But I still have fears that are coming up; I don't think my drain is totally unclogged yet." That's okay; even if there is a tiny opening where there used to be a complete blockage, that's enough to get the flow moving, and once the flow starts moving, it'll push through all of the other gross hair that's stuck in your drain. Really, if you can even see that there's a blockage, then your awareness is rising; that's huge progress. Most people don't even know that there is a bunch of tangled hair, toenail clippings, old Band-Aids, and Barbie dolls shoes blocking the connection to themselves.

We're moving into a place now where, because we are connected to being, we can start to take action in a way that is truly meaningful and connected to the whole. Now that we're going beyond the illusion, we're in a place where you can start to access your WHY, which we talked about in chapter sixteen. Now that our minds aren't trying to figure out HOW they're going to get something (so that they can create the illusion of safety), they're free to start actually creating in a totally original, unique, and spontaneous way.

When we're trying to create from our minds, we can only look at what we already know and what we've done before. We can mash concepts together and try to create something new, but whatever we create is, in many ways, just the repackaging of something that's been done before. It's like if a band was trying to make a hit song and they asked, "How do we make a hit?" They'd probably just listen to another song that was already a hit and try to make a song like that. Yeah, they might get close, and maybe that song could be good too, but since it's not a truly unique, inspired creation, it's doubtful that it would be one of those lasting hit songs that grab people in their hearts. Millions of songs have already been written, but an infinite number of songs haven't been written yet, so asking HOW and looking at past examples puts you in a very limited space. When Stevie Wonder writes music, you know that he's not trying to figure out what would be a hit song; you can tell he's just picking something up like an antenna and letting it come through. You can even see it in the way he moves: he's just swaying back and forth, hearing something no one else can.

So, for example, if you have a business, and you're asking yourself, "HOW should I market this thing?" you'll probably look at all the ways that other businesses have marketed things before. If you switch to "WHY do I want to market this?" you'll find an entirely new motivation that will give you access to new, innovative ideas. Or you might find that you don't have a WHY, which shows you that you're not marketing something that is truly a passion of yours. You might decide to switch gears and create something that is actually calling to you, which might feel scary at first but in the end will create way more internal alignment and allow you access to even more flow around it.

If you had the cure for cancer, you'd have a huge WHY. You'd have to get it out to the world because you'd know how much it would help people. There'd be no obstacle that could get in your way. That big of a WHY would allow the most effortless ideas for getting it out to the world to come to you.

You know you're in a WHY when the idea you have helps other people. We have this mysterious guidance in us that will always show us exactly how to do something if it's to help other people. And by "help other people," I mean help other people align with their souls and connect with themselves. I don't mean help other people by getting them to drink more Coca-Cola. Everything just seems to magically align when you're doing something that is selfless. When you're sharing something that is truly inspired and from your heart, you have to get that message out, and life will constantly open up doors for you to do that. As my good friend Michael Beckwith once said, "When you work for the universe, you're never unemployed."

So, if you're trying to get something for yourself, it's a HOW and will be a struggle. If you're helping other people, it's a WHY and will be effortless. You know that you're universally aligned when you're moving from a WHY.

This book started out being written in a HOW, which is why I was feeling closed off at first. Then it switched to a WHY, because I knew that you were getting something out of it and that I would grow more into my alignment, which will help me help the world. Moving to that WHY, and connecting to giving, opened up an infinite amount of content. We're here, like two hundred pages later, because I stopped doing this for myself and started doing it for you, which is also myself, as we established when you looked into your Photoshopped eyes.

Once you realize that you are here to become the WHY, HOW only shows up to support questions like "How can I give unconditionally?" or "How can I move like an apple tree?" You'll start to shift to a place where these types of questions are your conditioned patterns and you'll never ask a selfish HOW question again, because you'll start to learn that much more internal *and* external fulfillment comes from asking, "How can I give?"

The only thing the universe wants to do is give. It only wants to help others and bring them into alignment with universal principles so we can become the fullest expression of ourselves. The only thing it wants from us is for us to become that full expression. Until you connect to that universal truth where infinite love just wants to come through, you will be disconnected. In that disconnection, you will be forced to try to *get* using the strategy of your mind because you are cut off from the natural flow that is waiting for you as soon as you move in alignment with the cycle of giving that wants to happen through you.

Once you start giving from a WHY, you won't believe how many of the things that you wanted before will start to show up naturally. If you really want to get all of those things that you desire, shift to giving. If you don't see any results, that's because you're still trying to get. You need to truly surrender your "getting" and move to an infinite place of abundance and giving in order to tap into the flow of life that will provide you with everything you need. You've got to **make sure that you're not trying to give so that you can get**. That's low-vibrational giving, and if you are giving with the condition that you need to get something in return, you are very quickly going to deplete your resources. You need to give from your *infinite* *supply*, not your *limited supply*. Even if you don't have a lot of external resources, you have an infinite supply of things like creativity, compassion, and love. A simple way to evaluate this is: does it expand you to give, or does it deplete you to give?

Once you tap into, and eventually become, an infinite supply of gifts, you will be pulled off of the couch so that you can give those gifts to the world. Life will start to use you to your full potential. You won't have a choice.

If your reason for doing something is to just get more or be better than other people, that won't drive you. That will completely stifle you and constantly keep you in the practice of thinking that you're incomplete without the thing you think you need. Every mind-based HOW is only a solution to the problem *it created*. We can't move from a mind-based HOW because it will only be acknowledging that the false problem it created is real.

Don't get me wrong, the mind is capable of some amazing things and a lot of progress has been made from the cleverness of the mind, but the huge shifts, the social revolutions, the quantum leaps, have all come from a type of vision that can come only from a connection to the infinite imagination that just wants to give and express itself in bigger and bigger ways. The mind is only here to help coordinate everything that comes out of that vision. In this place, ideas can come out of nowhere and you start to act on inspiration without analyzing or questioning it because you trust that it knows something your mind can't see.

This is what I am doing all the time. When I walk out onstage, I have no idea what I'm going to say. The only way it works is that I stay in my WHY and allow something bigger than me to take over, and something fresh and new always comes out. Sure, sometimes I say things that I've said before, but because I'm open to possibility and I'm not planning with my mind from a strategy-based HOW, it always comes out different and I say new things I didn't know before I started. Living in that place of trust, and acting on it, allows me to be a portal for all of the insights I get to share with others. There is always an unlimited amount of information and inspiration just waiting for us to get into the internal alignment to access it.

Starting from a place of being and total acceptance is what allows that internal alignment to happen. That internal alignment is what creates the space for a powerful WHY to show up. We can never get the answer to something if we're trying to find it. We will never have an inspired idea if we are trying to *make* an inspired idea. Everything truly groundbreaking and innovative will come through in a moment when we let our guard down, connect to a place of giving, and finally let the intelligence of our souls come through.

What I've found is, the actual way to create results in your life is pretty much the exact opposite of everything that we have ever learned. We've learned that to create results you have to have a goal and work hard every day to achieve it. We've learned that we have to learn as much as possible and use our knowledge to become an expert on something to really succeed. We've learned that you have to create a burning desire for something for it to become a reality.

What *I've* experienced is, if you want something, you're not ready for it. If you believe that something outside of you is going to give you whatever feeling you've been searching for, you're living in a limited perspective that is cut off from the part of you that actually has the ability to accomplish whatever it is that you're trying to get.

Let me put it this way: If you really want to date someone, and you think that finally being able to date that person is going to make you happy, then you are stepping into the illusion that believes you are separate from the love and happiness that you actually are. In that separated place, you're trying to get something, and you'll be dependent on that person's reaction to you, so you'll start to manipulate yourself into being someone you think that person will like, but that won't be the authentic you. Because you're not being authentic and giving all of yourself, it makes it really hard for that person to be attracted to you. The fact that you want that person is the thing that might keep them from really connecting with you.

If, instead, you connect to yourself first and understand that no matter what happens, you are whole and complete, then you go into that date as the full expression of what you are and there's a much bigger possibility that the other person will be attracted to you. This is how I plan to date Jennifer Aniston. For me, this whole book was about learning how to do that.

In this place of total connection to yourself, some people will still not be attracted to you, and that might be because the love that you are connecting to within yourself is terrifying to someone who has spent their entire life looking for love outside of themselves. Basically, when you live in your heart, sometimes people who live in their heads will not feel worthy of being around you. This is how the universe pre-rejects people who don't align with your soul, so you can make room to only be around people who do. This is how you make real relationships, real friendships, and real business partnerships. In this alignment, you will only be around people who have the same expansive, loving passion for making the world better that you have. Now you don't have to connect on only the weather or football. You can connect on *you*.

This place of connection to ourselves and allowing a WHY to come through is the most important part of creating anything in your life. Like I said before though, you can't just use this state of being as a tool to get what you want. You can't trick the universe. It's the universe; it knows all about your bullshit. You have to actually step into something that you've never been before and learn how to tap into your unlimited giving. What you want will come as soon as you let go of the need for anything other than this connection to yourself. Then it will come in whatever way is most important for you. It might not even come in the form of something external that other people can see. It might just come to you in the form of an internal hole within you that is filled with the knowing that you already are whatever you have been looking for outside of yourself. Everything that we desire outside of ourselves is just a representation of something that we are not aware of or not acknowledging within ourselves.

So yeah, this place of being is absolutely the most important thing, but from that place, we now get to play in the sandbox of life while contributing in a way that we never were able to in a place of strategy and separation. We get to explore, express, and create an impact on the world in a richer and deeper way than the mind ever could, because the limitations that the mind has put on our experience are melting away.

Now we're going learn how to use the ego to our advantage.

We're still going to create amazing things, we're just going to start creating from a place of being. Instead of doing something to get to a goal, we're going to do something with the goal of just being on a journey with no end. So this isn't about removing goals or outcomes, it's about creating the goal of opening up to the infinite possibility in every moment, which can create a million different outcomes that are even better and more fulfilling than any external goal or HOW the mind could ever come up with.

None of this that I'm saying is "the way"; I'm just sharing what I've learned that has started to give me the freedom to truly play and create a new level of impact in this life. I just want to share this with everyone who is asking for it (that's my WHY).

So now we know we are ready to really tap into a crazy level of creativity and action, without the attachment to results or neediness we might have had before. Once you are living fully in a WHY, you can ask and receive the answer to "How?"

The rest of the book is going to be taking us into that next level of effortless creativity that will grab us and pull us into the insane amount of impact that we can truly make on this planet. We're going to discover that many skills, assets, and abilities *you already have* are actually in collaboration with each other, and that when combined with your WHY, they will give you the answer to every HOW that arises. Almost every want that you have will fall away and will be replaced with a NEED to give your gift and share with the world. And for those people who still need reassurance, yeah, we'll still get to make a bunch of money and all that stuff. Although, if you still need that reassurance, you should reread this book from like chapter fourteen on. And meditate a bunch too.

chapter 21

The Beginning of Abundance and the End of Disqualification

Okay, I want to show you something really cool. This is an exercise that is going to be the catalyst for something huge. What I mean by that is, this exercise is like mining raw materials so that we can make something really really amazing with them later. It's less dangerous than mining though . . . unless you do this exercise deep in a cave that has the possibility of collapsing; then it's equally dangerous.

Before you start, remember, this isn't about finding the right result, this is about getting you in the habit of tapping into your creativity, playing, and not disqualifying things that could be the gateway to new possibilities that your mind can't see. This exercise is a great opportunity to allow yourself to just start without knowing HOW. To do this, it's actually really helpful to not know the specifics or even why you're doing it, and to give yourself permission to just be on the journey without trying to figure out what it's leading to. Just allow yourself to go with whatever comes up, whenever it comes up.

This is a major aspect of how I live my life. All day I have ideas and inspirations that come up and I have no idea why I'm supposed to do those things. Sometimes it even seems like doing those things would steer me away from my overall goal, but when I follow a feeling in my body that makes me excited to do something, it often leads me down a path where I can accomplish that goal, or an even bigger thing, way faster than I would have otherwise. Every time you get excited about something without knowing the specifics, go with it. That excitement is the universe giving you a WHY. It's a step toward freeing universal expression, it's a step toward contribution, it's a step toward growth.

One of our biggest problems is we disqualify the ideas that come through all day long because they don't fit the mold of what our minds think is possible based on our limited pasts. Even though we might have hundreds of original, inspired ideas coming through every day, we immediately negate them because we're more afraid of stepping out of the fearful story of ourselves than taking a chance on our own expansion. Sometimes an idea will come up and we can't see the entire picture of it right away, so we dismiss it because we don't understand the bigger thing it was leading us to. If we would just go with that idea on faith, we would understand, later, everything that was trying to emerge from that one small inspiration. Eventually, you'll realize that feeling is even more practical and provable than what we think of as "having faith." As you keep doing this, it's not blind faith anymore. You will start to give yourself 100 percent proof that those excited feelings are leading you to something huge. Having that feeling is like having your own life coach living in your body, telling you the next step, and the only proof you need is that it feels better to follow those inspirations.

It's like when Benjamin Franklin had the idea to fly a kite, and there was something inside of him that was just excited to go fly a kite, even though it was raining, and he just followed that inspired idea and then invented electricity. I'm sure that's not how that story goes, but if you just go with it, it really works for this example. Seriously though, how many times can you think of in your life where one thing led you to something bigger that you never would have discovered had you not done that first thing? When we start to follow more of these inspired ideas without attachment to the results of any one thing, that kind of synchronicity gets exponential and you end up in an entirely different world of possibility. All it took was a series of small, effortless, and guided steps. And a kite. The point of this chapter is to get a kite, and then you too can invent electricity and peanut butter. I know that was a different guy, but I'm sure he used a kite to do it.

I remember one time, it was a few weeks before an Evolving Out Loud event and I went to a place that I love called Asilomar in Monterey, California. I remember, in my head, wanting to get back home so that I could work out a lot and get in great shape before the event, but my body just wanted to stay in Asilomar and relax. So I went with that feeling, which was much more exciting—not because it was easier, it just felt better somehow. So I just chilled for a few more days and ate whatever I felt like. I hardly worked out at all, but weirdly, I lost a bunch of weight. As I let go of the old story of my trying to get somewhere, my body actually got even healthier than it probably would have if I had worked my ass off at the gym, just by relaxing.

What I couldn't see in the story of my mind is that the weight I was trying to lose by going to the gym was really there because I was holding on to this idea that I needed to look a certain way or do a certain thing so that I could get love. When I let that story go, my body was able to let go and the pounds just flew off. I know that if I had worked out three or four times a day, it wouldn't have even compared to following my highest excitement and connecting to myself as that old part of my identity fell away. Also, the content that I was able to share at the event was so much deeper because I was so universally aligned and less trying to "get it right." The event going well rippled out in the form of impact on other people, You-Tube videos that went viral, more fans, and so many other things that weren't contained in the feeling that I should just hang out in Asilomar. You'd think that to accomplish all of that, you'd have to really prepare a lot and work really hard, but it was even more effective to just relax and connect with a deeper calling in myself.

So, our first job is to stop disqualifying the things that our hearts are pulling us toward. We're going to enter a space of allowing every single thing that comes up (externally and internally). We're going to be in a space of letting ourselves feel what we need to feel, hear what we need to hear, and create what we need to create to grow into our next stage of expansion. We can't control the thoughts and ideas that come up, but we can allow ourselves to go with them and let them guide us into whatever is necessary for our own evolution. We don't need to know all the specifics, we don't need to complete anything immediately, we just need to open up the doorway and start allowing everything to come through that wants to come through.

So, this is an exercise that I do with clients that shows them how much abundance and how many different assets they have in their lives that they might be overlooking. This isn't really about creating a list of things to make you feel abundant, although that will happen. This is more about learning how to go with the flow and starting to move your awareness into a place that can see higher-level possibilities than you might be used to.

This exercise will feel amazing as you do it. Your WHY for doing this exercise isn't about any results that it will bring; your WHY is just that it feels good. Because it feels good, it means that everything you learn while doing this exercise will be used to help contribute to the world later. This is something that we need to get used to: following those things that feel good, and knowing that everything that feels good in our soul is leading us to a bigger level of impact and expression in the world. No matter what the thing is, if it calls to you in your heart, it will reveal a new expansion in you that will either prepare you for or lead you to the next step in your journey. Now let's take that step.

So for this exercise, take out another piece of paper or grab your notebook. You should remember what paper is from the left-and-right-page exercise in chapter seventeen. There were like four different pictures explaining how to use paper. You should definitely remember.

So on this new piece of paper, first, you're going to **write down all the assets that you have right now in your life**.

We have so many assets that we don't even realize are assets. It's amazing how often we discount our abilities and focus on what we *don't* have instead of what we *do* have. No matter who you are or where you are, you have hundreds of assets, whether you know it or not. If you've made it this far into the book, that's an asset! If you've done that, then you have awareness (which is actually the most valuable asset of all). You also have the ability to read. You also have the ability to stick with something. You probably also have a sense of humor, unless you hate the jokes in this book. In which case, you have the ability to ignore jokes that you hate in order to get more awareness, which is also an asset.

What other assets do you have? Your friends are an asset. Friends of your friends are assets. Facebook is an asset. YouTube is an asset. You might have a cell phone; that's an asset. Your cell phone might record video; that's an asset. If you've got all of those things, then an asset you have right now is that you can record a video, post it on Facebook or YouTube, and share it with all of your friends, who might in turn share it with their friends. When we're aware of all of these seemingly insignificant assets that we have in each moment, we can start to take action on more and more of those ideas that pop into our head, allowing results to start piling up. I don't know how many times some insight or idea has shown up, and because I'm aware of assets like these, I've immediately just made a video and posted it. It takes me ten minutes and the video lives on forever. That opportunity happens billions of times a day all around the globe, but only a fraction of those ideas are acknowledged and acted on.

So what else? You really have an infinite number of assets, whether external or internal, that are important ingredients to your unique creative expression. So on this piece of paper, just let all of them pour out. No filter. No second-guessing. Even things that you might be thinking of as negative may actually be assets. If you've broken up with someone, you have the experience of that as an asset to draw on. If you like to gossip, that's an asset that might get you a job on the E! channel or something. My point is, ALL YOU ARE is an asset. Everything you've ever experienced, failed at, achieved, learned, or unlearned is an asset that you can draw on when you're in a place of possibility.

So I challenge you to write down at least one hundred assets that you currently have in your life *right now*, no matter how obvious or obscure they might be.

Okay, now the next thing we're going to look at is all the assets that are available to you but that you might not have right this second. For example, you have the ability to get to Oprah. You might not know her right now, but Oprah can absolutely become an asset of yours, once you get in the alignment for her to be an asset. This exercise is about creating that alignment. If you get down to it, the only reason Oprah isn't already an asset of yours is because you haven't seen yourself as someone who is worthy of Oprah's being an asset to you. That's because you haven't accessed this understanding of your unlimited assets and value enough to create an equal give-and-take for Oprah. When you do that and allow a powerful WHY to move you and all of your infinite assets into action, you'll be in an alignment where you and Oprah's working together would be an even exchange for both of you. Obviously, Oprah is a general example, but the same principle applies to every single thing or opportunity that you might want. All you have to do is raise yourself to the alignment where it would feel normal for you to have it.

You also have the ability to make billions of dollars; you just haven't created the alignment for billions of dollars to come to you yet. Understanding all of the other assets that are available to you is the first step to unlocking the ability to receive the ideas and inspiration that could allow you to create billions of dollars' worth of value.

So what are all the assets that, if you raised your alignment, you could access? This list is REALLY infinite. There is not a person or organization or resource on this planet that you couldn't bring yourself into alignment with as you access the unlimited potential that you have inside of yourself. Seriously, start thinking BIG here. Not only is this your opportunity to stretch your vision of what you can bring to the world, but it's also your opportunity to understand that you are not this limited fear story that tells you that you're unworthy of anything or anyone. If you put down an asset but hear a voice tell you that it's impossible to be in alignment with it, realize you're listening to an illusion. Realize that voice is a fictional character that is invested in keeping you in a lower alignment because it's afraid. Write down that asset anyway.

So with this list, I challenge you to **write down another one hundred assets that will be available to you when you step into your true value.** Remember, as you write all this stuff down, you're going to have things come up that might seem silly or way out there, but they only seem silly based on your judgment. Your job is to not disqualify them. No matter how stupid it might sound, write it down. If it came up, it's valid.

Okay, what else do you have? What skills have you gained throughout your life? Let's **do another list with one hundred skills that you have**. I realize you might have written some skills in the first asset list, but I want you to go as deep as possible with this exercise. Can you ride a bike? Are you bilingual? Do you know how to sit in a chair? That might sound stupid, but one of my clients once wrote down that they knew how to sit in a chair as one of their skills, and we ended up riffing on that and creating a comedy sketch video where he taught people how to sit in a chair. It was amazing. Every one of these skills and assets is a thread that you can pull that will unravel an entire new set of options for creativity.

Okay, fourth list. In this list we're going to write down one hundred things that you love. You might say "my mom." You might say "Kyle Cease." You might say "the beach." Everything that you love about this life, I want you to put on this list. How often do we actually sit and think about everything that we love? If nothing else, the gratitude for life that you will feel during this part of the exercise is enough to make the whole thing worth it. Spend time and savor this one. Every single thing that you love, no matter how big or small, put it down. Remember, reading this and not doing it is like having someone explain to you how an elliptical machine works. Doing it is getting on the elliptical machine. You will experientially shift as you actually do this.

Here we go, fifth list. I bet you thought that last list was the last one. Nope. There's this one too. The fifth list is all about everything that you know and understand from your experiences. What have you been through that has taught you something that someone else might not know? What have you learned from life? What are things that you'd want to share with people? What are some of the experiences that have impacted your life? There's nothing that you've been through in your life that hasn't contributed to who you are today. Every single experience you've had is an asset.

This book is a product of all of my life experience. Because I can see the value in my experience, it's allowed me to share it with you and write hundreds of pages about it. You are no different than me. You've had millions of experiences that have taught you so much too, but you might have disqualified them and thought, "No one would want to read what I have to say." If you can find the value in something you've experienced, I promise other people will too. If you just go with the feeling of whatever comes up and write it down, you'll learn what the value is as you do it. So I dare you to **write down one hundred things that you know based on experiences that you've had in your life**.

Okay, the next ten lists are where this exercise really heats up . . . I'm just kidding. That was the last list.

So now you should have five hundred different assets, future assets, skills, things you love, and things that you know written down. Now, when you look at these lists, what I really want to emphasize to you is *do not* disqualify them. It might not make sense right now how all of those things relate, but don't worry about that.

Right now, just acknowledge how abundant, how skilled, how valuable you are, and realize that all of that is going to come together in an even more amazing way to bring you into more purpose, more passion, and more impact. The next chapter is going to be taking all of these raw materials and guiding you into the next steps to start moving from your heart and acting on the calling of your soul. Remember, even though these assets and different ideas that are coming up are important, they are really just catalysts for you to be in the practice of realizing that you are a fountain and that you have access to an infinite number of assets and possibilities. When you align with your WHY and tap into universal creativity it will skyrocket your impact, income, health, relationships . . . it will change everything.

chapter 22

Surrounded by Excitement

So, what I want to do for the next part of this exercise is to take the "light vs. heavy feeling" concept that we've talked about already and apply that to these assets that you've written down. I want to give you the opportunity to practice listening to and following what feels good and what feels bad in your body. As I talked about before, there is an immediate knowing that you have in every moment that is giving you all the information you could ever need; this part of the exercise is going to be training yourself to hear and act on that knowing.

Here's how we're going to do that: Look at everything you wrote down. As you go down your list, one at a time, pay attention to how each thing you wrote down makes you feel on a scale of one to ten. So, with one being the heaviest and ten being the lightest, you're going to write down where each thing you wrote down falls on that scale. You have to be willing to make these ratings almost instantly. This isn't the time to sit and consider if it's heavy or light; this is an opportunity to allow that instinctual knowing inside of you to be heard and acknowledged. That instinctual knowing will tell you immediately whether it feels heavy or light. Within the first second, either you will feel stressed and in your head when you look at something that feels heavy, or you'll feel excited and expansive (sometimes even a little scared) when you look at something that is light.

You don't have to explain the things that are *supposed* to be in your life. Remember from earlier, when you're justifying or explaining something, you don't actually want to do or have that thing in your life. Many people are in jobs or relationships, or other situations, where they have to keep justifying to themselves why they stay in them, which means their hearts don't really want to be there. Even though their heads can come up with a bunch of logical reasons why it might make sense to stay there, their hearts know that they're actually limiting themselves and their contributions to the world by staying. This is not me telling you to quit your job or break up with your spouse, this is just me reminding you that you have the answer inside of you for every decision you need to make, and if you follow it, you will effortlessly drop the things that are keeping you from accessing your true power while moving you toward freedom. So, if you're justifying anything on your list, know that it's heavy for you. You are learning to follow the feeling, not the reason. From now on, *the feeling is the reason*.

So in this exercise, I want you to just get in the practice of following the feeling by rating each one of your assets from that instinctual place in your gut, not from the analytical logic of your mind. For everything that feels like a nine or ten and immediately gives you a feeling of excitement without any justification, circle it. There might be some things that you wrote down that you're really good at or that make you a lot of money, but when you tune into your internal guidance, you might find out that those things don't excite you at all. You might have been coasting on the justification of your mind while your body has been screaming at you to drop that thing and move toward something that moves you more into alignment with life and taps into your ability to contribute. That voice is always there; we don't have to work to find it. In this exercise, we're just bypassing the noise of the mind that makes it hard to hear that voice most of the time.

This is about trusting that guidance that you have within you and finally allowing yourself to acknowledge what your true passions are, without having to give any reasons why you want to do those things. One of your passions could be walking in the park. Your mind might say that you don't have time for that or it's not going to create income, but if you're excited to do it, then you can know that moving on that excitement will create some result that allows you to expand into a new place. You might just feel more relaxed from walking into a park and it'll allow a new idea to come through that you wouldn't have had otherwise. You might meet someone in the park that you start a relationship with. You might pick up a kite and invent electricity. All of those, especially the last one, are 100 percent possibilities that your soul might be calling you toward by giving you that simple feeling of excitement when you think about them. We've been talking about trusting throughout this entire book, and this exercise will allow you to let that calling come through so it can give you the evidence of your alignment in a million different ways.

So go ahead now and look through your list and just allow your body/your heart/your soul to tell you what are the assets that are effortless and exciting to you. If you catch yourself having to think about it for a few seconds, you already know that's not a nine or ten. Your nines and tens will jump out at you with no effort on your part. Allow yourself to totally give up control and let your body tell you what the next step is, kind of like using a Ouija board, but hopefully less terrifying. When you're done, go to the next chapter, where we'll ask Abraham Lincoln questions about the afterlife.

chapter 23

Your Biggest Asset

You have now put together a huge list of assets, skills, experiences, and opportunities in your life that you have been overlooking, and you have reminded yourself about all of the things that you love within that list. This list is here so that you can understand how much opportunity you are surrounded by in every moment. The only job that you have, without understanding why, is to take the things on your list that excite you, and anything else that might come up, and surround yourself with them. Eliminate the things that don't excite you in your body. When you do this, you will rise to an overall higher vibration that will allow you to appreciate and receive on an entirely new level.

If it's not something that you circled on your list and doesn't make you feel lighter in your body when you think about it, it's not your highest calling. Feel free to delegate those things or do whatever you have to do so that you can spend the twenty-four hours that you have each day surrounded with the things that make you feel unbelievable and expansive. You will start acting more on your creativity and the infinite amount of potential that is available when you do only what you love and start truly living in a WHY. Your WHY is to evolve, your WHY is to expand, your WHY is to free yourself.

Even though this might seem like an arbitrary list of amazing-feeling things, all of these can be combined to create different careers, passions, and projects that have the opportunity to make a tremendous impact on the world. If you look at this list from a high enough perspective, you'll discover the common thread that is weaving all of your unique talents and gifts into something that life has been waiting all of eternity to express through you.

I've made a new life out of combining comedy and transformation. I also love improv, being playful, growing, music, and entertaining people. The events that I do combine every one of those things. Those passions were all seemingly unrelated parts of my original list of assets, and I had no idea that they would come together and create something that is so beneficial to myself and others. I just had to look at all of my skills, not disqualify anything, and be open to possibility, and something more powerful and impactful than anything I could have planned came out of it. I don't do the accounting. I don't do the video editing. I put my attention only on the things that I love and that allow me to be the most *me* possible. Yes, the accounting needs to be done, but there is someone else who loves to do that. If I spend some of my time doing some of the things that I don't love, then it will negatively affect the time I spend with the things I do love. My friend Glenn Morshower said, "If you pee in one part of the pool, you pee in all of the pool." This is why I prefer hot tubs.

The most important asset you have is your ability to consistently live in the high vibration of excitement. When you're in that high vibration of excitement, you realize that everything is working together and nothing is in conflict.

One of the things that causes us pain in our lives is that we compartmentalize and separate everything instead of bringing all of our assets into collaboration. You can have an amazing business and allow everything in your life to support and inspire that business, instead of taking away from it. You could have your spouse help you with ideas, you could bring your kids to work, and you could find an unlimited number of ways to bring everything you love into it. Your business can, and should, be an extension of the things you love *instead of cutting you off from them.*

You're not here to get to an end point; **your end point is to be in an open-ended possibility.** When you just become this giant space of possibility that anything can come through, you start to realize that all of your life is interconnected. Waking up and brushing my teeth is somehow connected to when I go onstage. The drive to the venue becomes content for the stage. When I'm finally onstage, it's just another moment that is spilling into the next.

Because I know that every single thing is connected to everything else, I can't even take credit for the things that I do. Someone else taught me English so that I could communicate this to others. Someone else made the car that I drive so I could get to the venue.

Someone else made the food that I ate before I went on. Someone else made the clothes that I wore so people could focus on my eyes instead of on my abs. Thank god I also have six-pack eyes.

Every single thing that I do consists of the contributions of literally thousands of other people. Knowing that allows me to let go of control and just ride the wave of creation that started way before I even got here. Something bigger than us is taking care of all of these countless details so that we can experience this moment and expand into the limitless possibilities that exist in it.

Stepping into the things that are light and exciting to you will raise your vibration so that you can start to actually experience what I'm talking about here. Life will start to transform, and instead of seeing all the problems and the reasons why you can't do something, you'll just see green lights and all of the exciting opportunities for your expansion.

Following these inspirations will give other people permission to start letting go of the heavy things in their lives so they can move into their possibility too, and then you'll be part of the ripple effect that is transforming this planet and our society before our eyes.

By doing this, you will continuously expand into a life that is a never-ending journey of possibility, versus just moving toward the endgame of making as much money as you can so you can retire and work on your hot sauce collection. You're here to live in the unknown and experience the excitement of discovering something new in every moment as you bring more and more love into the world. Doesn't that sound fun?

chapter 24

You Are Completely Free.
Act Like It.

You are completely free. Not just because you've read this book; you've actually been free the entire time. Even if you feel completely isolated and trapped in your circumstances, you are totally free. Even if you are in a prison, you are 100 percent free. Everything you've read in this book has just been a reminder to help pull you out of the false belief that you are not.

We have created the illusion that to be free, we have to make our external situations free. We believe that we need to live in a free country, but the country you live in is a perfect mirror of the level of freedom that exists within its citizens. If *every* aspect of any country became completely free, its population would freak out and that level of freedom would probably cause even more fear and chaos. We're not ready to live in a *completely free* society yet because we're not, as individuals, *completely free* internally. We have trained ourselves to give our power away to whatever we can find outside of ourselves. Until we look inward, we will demand to be ruled by everything external to ourselves.

We love to worship other people, money, careers, astrology, ideologies, our fears, a judgmental mind-made god, teachers, the stock market, the news, celebrities, addictions, our parents, our friends, opinions . . . but we very rarely worship *ourselves*. Until we do this, we will never be free.

When you have an insightful idea, don't get excited about the idea. Get excited about YOU, because the idea came from YOU. You are the source of the idea. If you freak out about the idea, you'll be like an apple tree screaming about an apple that it made. As it gets excited about this one apple, it will stop making more.

When you have a fear-based thought, realize that this thought came from you too. You are the source of the thought, and now you are in resistance to your own thought. This is like painting a picture of a monster, forgetting you painted it, putting it up on the wall, then freaking out every night because of this picture that YOU made.

If you have been working in a job that you don't like or you're in a relationship that stifles you, YOU are choosing imprisonment now while demanding that things outside of you change for your freedom. If you are in any situation that you don't like, you can leave it if you want to, RIGHT NOW. But if you are choosing it, that is because you are choosing to make your external world match the limitations of your internal world. You will never be free by *only* changing the external world.

The biggest reason that we stress is because we are trying to control the things that we can't control and aren't controlling what we can. There are so many things that we can't directly control. We can't control what a football team just did. We can't control our past. We can't control what other people think about us. However, we love to grab on to these situations and argue with them because we can't do anything about it.

We *can* control our decisions. We *can* control our intention. We *can* control who and what we surround ourselves with. But **the biggest thing we *can* control is . . . whether or not we accept this moment fully.** This moment that you are in right now, do you accept it completely? Do you accept *all* of your emotions? Do you accept all of your past and future? Do you accept what they said about you? Do you accept that things might have been working against your expectations? Do you? If you do, you will move forward into a place within yourself that will allow you to start cocreating with life in a magical way, and the new world that you want to live in will start to show up around you.

There are millions of opportunities available to you that could match the freedom that you actually are. There are innovative careers, loving relationships, healthy foods, and expansive habits that are completely available to you right now, in this moment. You have the opportunity in this actual second to step into more freedom. The question is, will you take it?

Will you free yourself through showing up and staying in the room? Through meditation? Through leaping? Through letting go of heavy things? Through melting? Through acting on your left-page excitement? Through tapping into your apple tree and listening to your calling? Through controlling only what you can? Through appreciating and acknowledging all of the unlimited assets you have available to you? Through surrounding yourself with only what you love?

When you realize and embody that you are 100 percent free, you understand that nothing can stop you anymore. No circumstance is bigger than you, and you will be able to move effortlessly with every single thing that's happening. I have heard other speakers say this sentence, but as time goes on and you start to embody this knowing, you **start to see the world the way god sees it.**

You remove the part of you that thinks something bad is happening to you. You start to see that every aspect of life is completely in sync with you. You start to see that all of your judgments were based only on fear and that there is always a higher perspective that loves every situation.

When I speak at my two-day events, sometimes it seems like there are things going wrong. Sometimes the video screen doesn't work. Sometimes a person freaks out and runs up onto the stage. Sometimes a heckler will totally start talking out of turn and try to change the schedule around. When any of this happens, I GO WITH IT. It's all an opportunity to make a masterpiece by cocreating with the universe and trusting that everything is happening for a reason. All of those things that go "wrong" suddenly become a huge part of the event and end up being so entertaining that the audience almost thinks we set up those "mistakes" on purpose.

Everything that goes "wrong" in your life is your opportunity to improvise and cocreate YOUR MASTERPIECE with the universe.

We know that "life is a gift," but what we don't hear is that YOU ARE A GIFT FOR LIFE TOO. Life needs you to bring the infinite power that you are into this world. Life needs your compassion, your creativity, your unconditional acceptance, your heart, and your patience to flow through you to create this new world that is based on peace, love, kindness, and giving. This is all available and it LITERALLY STARTS WITH YOU. You cannot control what others do. But you can control what you do. You can let go of the heaviness of the world and grab on to the infinite lightness of your intentions.

I did not write this book in order to create a bunch of followers. I wrote this for my expansion and I am wide open to the idea that my expansion is giving you permission to access your expansion. I get excited about the idea of having a bunch of colleagues who are here with me, like business partners accessing our highest gifts to make the world better.

I can't believe that all of this unfolded for me. I am taking a second and feeling so proud of myself and in awe of what I have learned and embodied through writing this book. I can't believe there was a time when I was considering bailing on this. I can't believe I was so scared. I can't believe this new awareness has shown up for me simply by staying in the room. I feel a whole new excitement about life and had I not written this, I would not have known about any of this. I would be staying in the sad comfort of my imaginary limitations, thinking that I am some little separate piece of ice who can't do things. But because I did the thing, I proved to myself that I am so much more than I ever knew. I hope you are discovering that for yourself too.

The most important thing of all is . . .

OH SHIT. I just did a word count and discovered that as of the end of this sentence, we are going to be at 59,999 words!

THE

Acknowledgments

Boy, I have no idea how to start acknowledgments. I have a lot of people in my life who mean the world to me. I guess I have to start with my fiancée, Christy Harden, who started dating me after this book was written (you snooze, you lose, Aniston). She will probably not be my fiancée by the time you finish this book (hopefully because we got married). Every time I look into her eyes, my heart hurts a little because the love I feel for her is beyond anything I have ever known, and it's really uncomfortable.

I have to thank Dan McKim for supporting me fully and helping me put this book together. My team is absolutely amazing, and I couldn't do anything without them. Norm Aladjem is the manager who believed in me completely and became one of my closest friends. Kari Geddes, the greatest, most loving space on the planet who completely helped to cocreate and develop Evolving Out Loud and is always there twenty-four hours a day. EVEN AT NOON!

I want to write sentences about each person but it will take a while. The rest of my team: Sanaz Yamin, Kara Hamilton, Chris Taylor, Kailey Waite, Heather Smith, and everyone ever involved with EOL. Thank you to Richard and Michele Cohn for getting me in front of Michele Martin. Thank you to Michele Martin for listening to Richard and

Michele, and then talking to Norm, then waiting a week, and then talking to Sanaz and then Norm again. Then I think you spoke to Richard and Michele again. Then Norm's assistant, then Norm. Then a conference call with all of us.

Now I have to jump to my best friend of all time "Justin Ison." I have no idea why I put his name in quotes. I totally believe that's his name.

My brother, Kevin Cease, a die-hard seeker of life, who inspires me constantly and who is a master of not caring what others think. To my friends Angela Matesky Ertel, Bryan Reeves, Jason Moffatt, Kelly Carlin, Renee Adams, Sara Williams, James Mellon, Glenn Morshower, Lindsay Heller, Jeff Marx, David Wolfe, Gail Kingsbury, Beth Ison, Wendy Newman, Cori Dixon, Barb Millorn, Mark Dejoy, Mike Kemski, Abe Smith, Scott Carlin, Diego Attanasio, Christie Blogsdale. . . . I am scared I made this list so big because now more people will be mad that I didn't mention them.

My dear lifelong friend Amanda Richardson, who has one of the biggest hearts on this planet.

To my friend Louise Palanker, who talked my dad into driving me into Hollywood on Christmas Day when I was fifteen.

My mom has always been the carrot at the end of the stick. Nancy Cease is someone who was so awesome to me that getting her approval has always been a driving force. Luckily I had to earn her approval, and I just got it this year, so I will probably quit everything now.

When I was a kid, I watched my dad, Alan Cease, create numerous companies out of thin air. This inspired me to always remember that I could do whatever I wanted, so I did it.

To my grandma Bea, my uncle John, my grandpa Ernie, my grandma Genie, Sara, Alison, Devin, Andrew, and the rest of my actively loving, creative family members who lived their calling right in front of me.

I have so many inspirations. Michael Beckwith, Bob Proctor, Louis C.K., Jim Carrey, Steve Martin, Byron Katie, Billy Joel, Dr. Sue Morter, Mikki Willis, Eckhart Tolle, Ellen DeGeneres, India.Arie, Jack Canfield, and so many others. To everyone who has shown up in my life. Whether our experience felt good or bad, it was part of my experience and it made me better. I don't have much to say about Janet Reno, as she was never a direct part of my life.

Foreword, backward

The late, heart-centered comedian Robin Williams once said, "Comedy is acting out optimism." Mark Twain put it this way: "Humor is mankind's greatest blessing." It's no wonder, then, that Kyle Cease began his professional career as a comedian, for as is abundantly evident throughout this book, his optimism and humor are highly effective medicines for the human spirit. If there is one outstanding truth among the many within these pages, it's that one's calling in life is an ever-evolving expression of oneself. It is this realization that inspired Kyle to turn deeply within and shine the searchlight on how to deliver his gifts, talents, and skills as a source of inspiration and encouragement to his readers, as well as those who attend his Evolving Out Loud events. Through written expression of his personal growth, Kyle vulnerably shares with us how he came to combine humor with transformation, which has become a healing tool for millions of individuals.

Great teachers, such as the Buddha, many Hindu sages, and Jesus, to name a few, have encouraged us to be fully present in the now-moment, to remain attentive, awake, and aware. And for good reason, for it is being mindfully conscious—not self-conscious, which is ego-related—that stands us before the cosmic mirror in which we can catch the reflection of our Original Face. When through these means we cultivate the courage to look straight into ourselves, we become the calm, wise seer of our true life path. And just as it did for Kyle, the mind chatter of childhood conditioning falls away as we begin to dis-identify with its emotional noise and stop catering to its demands. At first this can feel like unfamiliar territory, causing us to ask, "Is this the real me?" But when our analytical mind stops defining the boundaries of who we think we are or who we should be, the deepest and most authentic Self begins to emerge.

The encouragement you will receive from Kyle's personal journey begins with the wisdom of no longer rejecting parts of yourself, with embracing with loving-kindness that you are the vast space of consciousness that holds it all. Feelings of fear, sadness, anxiety—when they are not rejected and instead experienced for the self-revelations they offer—no longer are regarded as enemies but rather as signposts guiding us to the next step in our evolutionary growth. We then begin to welcome all the beauty of what it means to be alive and all the pure, creative intelligence and unconditional love that is our inheritance.

I share from personal experience that when Kyle speaks at the Revelation Conference, which is hosted by the Agape International Spiritual Center, the organization I founded, the energy in the room is vibrant with joy; it becomes filled with authentic soul-laughter. The self-awareness into which he escorts us will also escort you, dear reader, into a deep intimacy with yourself.

Michael Bernard Beckwith
Author of Spiritual Liberation and Life Visioning
February 22, 2017, Los Angeles, California